JUNE & JULY

Make the Most of Every Month with Carson-Dellosa's Monthly Books!

Production Manager
Chris McIntyre

Editorial Director
Jennifer Weaver-Spencer

Writers
Lynette Pyne
Amy Gamble
Susan Yelvington
Georgia Butcher, Joan Daniels,
Julie Eick Granchelli,
L. Marie Lavallee, Linda Ludlow,
Karen Smith, Trisha Yates

Editors
Kelly Gunzenhauser
Maria McKinney
Carol Layton

Art Directors
Penny Casto
Alain Barsony

Art Coordinator
Edward Fields

Illustrators
Mike Duggins
Erik Huffine
David Lackey
Ray Lambert
Bill Neville
Betsy Peninger
J.J. Rudisill
Pam Thayer
Todd Tyson
Julie Webb

Cover Design
Amber Kocher Crouch
Ray Lambert
J.J. Rudisill

Carson-Dellosa Publishing Company, Inc.

JUNE & JULY

Table of Contents

JUNE/JULY TEACHER TIPS

Window Displays
As the weather gets warmer and children become more restless, help end outside distractions using a student-made ocean display. Cut blue construction paper into wave shapes and use the waves to cover the bottom portion of your classroom windows. Let students draw and cut out ocean animals and seashells, and attach them to the paper.

Storing Displays
When putting away bulletin boards and other displays at the end of the year, attach a resealable bag to the back of the largest bulletin board piece to hold letters and other small pieces. Take a photo of the display to place in the pocket for a reference to use when recreating the display the following year.

Keep in Touch
Let your students send you summer greetings. Write your address on an unlined 4" x 6" index card and add a postage stamp. Send the card home on the last day of school, along with a note asking students to write notes and mail the cards to you to tell you about their summertime activities.

Know at a Glance
Save yogurt containers with clear, dome-shaped topping holders and use them to store small craft items, glitter, or manipulatives. Fill the container with the items, then place a few in the clear top portion to help you identify at a glance what is inside the container.

Game Storage
Organize and store manipulatives and small games in cardboard filing cabinets. Label the outside of each drawer with its contents and a picture. When a student uses the manipulatives or games, have him remove the drawer, take it to the work area, and replace it when finished.

Gallons of Space
Large, empty ice cream containers from ice cream parlors make durable, roomy storage containers. Ask a local business to donate their empty ice cream containers with lids. Wash the containers and use them to store stuffed toys, puppets, or other items.

June

Day-by-Day Calendar

1 *Italian Heritage Month* Since pasta is the national food of Italy, make pasta necklaces with the class.

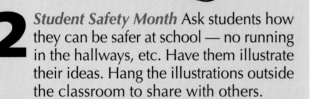

2 *Student Safety Month* Ask students how they can be safer at school — no running in the hallways, etc. Have them illustrate their ideas. Hang the illustrations outside the classroom to share with others.

3 *International Volunteers Week* Ask students to vote on volunteer groups that they think support the most worthwhile causes such as The Red Cross or Greenpeace. Then, write a class thank-you letter to the winner.

4 The *Heimlich Maneuver* was introduced by Henry J. Heimlich on this day in 1974. Have a CPR instructor demonstrate this lifesaving technique.

5 *National Family Day* Have students bring in pictures of family members to share with the class. Then, post the pictures on a bulletin board titled *We Love our Families*.

6 *National Hug Holiday Week* is June 6-12. Have the class make *Free Hug* coupons to give to friends or family members.

7 The *VCR* was introduced on this day in 1975. Survey the class to see if they prefer watching movies in a theater or with a TV and VCR.

8 *National Frozen Yogurt Month* Provide regular and frozen yogurt for a class taste-test. Give children squares of construction paper on which to write why they preferred the regular or frozen yogurt. Create a bar graph by having students group and assemble the squares on a bulletin board.

9 *Donald Duck's Birthday* This Disney duck was "born" today in 1934. Have students draw comic strips that include cartoon ducks.

10 *Maurice Sendak's Birthday* The author of *Where the Wild Things Are* was born in 1928. Ask students to draw pictures of their own imaginary "wild thing" monsters.

11 *Accordion Awareness Month* Teach the class some facts about this unique instrument. For example, the accordion is a portable keyboard that is considered a wind instrument.

12 *Adopt a Shelter Cat Month* On a large piece of butcher paper, have students create a banner urging others to support this cause. Have them draw pictures and write or dictate anecdotes about cats. Donate the banner to a local animal shelter for display.

13 June is *Turkey Lovers' Month* Have students brainstorm foods that contain turkey.

14 *National Candy Month* Have students name their favorite candies, then graph the results.

15 *National Iced Tea Month* Iced tea comes in many flavors such as regular, raspberry, peach, etc. Ask students to invent a new flavor of iced tea. What would it taste like? What would it be called?

16 *Valentina Tereshkova* became the *first woman in space* on this day in 1963. Have students draw today's rocket ships or space stations.

17 The *first National Spelling Bee* was *held* on this day in 1925. Hold a class spelling bee with weekly spelling words.

18 The *first American woman, Sally Ride, went into space today in 1983.* Write tongue twisters promoting her travels, such as *Sally Ride rode in a rapid rocket.*

19 *National Juggling Day* Show students how to juggle two balls. Then, let them practice juggling.

20 *Dairy Month* Vote on dairy products – cheese, ice cream, etc., to feature at snack time each week. Then, bring enough for all to share.

21 *Summer Solstice* Today is the first day of summer and the longest day of the year. Have students draw pictures that illustrate summertime fun.

22 *Zoo and Aquarium Month* Arrange a field trip to a local zoo or aquarium or have students illustrate pictures of the animals found in each.

23 The *saxophone* was *patented* on this day in 1846. Share music featuring this instrument with the class.

24 The *first recorded reports of flying saucers* were made on this day in 1947. Have students write an imaginary story about aliens they meet in their back yards.

25 The *table fork* was *introduced to America* on this day in 1630 by John Winthrop, governor of Massachusetts. Have students make a list of foods they eat with a fork. Then, ask them what they think it would be like to eat these foods without a fork.

26 *Charlotte Zolotow's Birthday* This famous children's author was born on this day in 1916. Share one of her books, such as *I Know a Lady*, with the class.

27 *Happy Birthday to You* was published on this day in 1924. It was written by Mildred and Patty Hill. Have students think of other lyrics that could be used with this famous tune.

28 *Fresh Fruit and Vegetable Month* Have students research which fruits and vegetables are planted and/or harvested in June.

29 *Fireworks Safety Month* Stress to students the dangers of playing with fireworks. Then, have them make posters about fireworks safety.

30 *Twins Foundations Founding* The primary research information center on twins was established today in 1983. Teach the class some facts about twins. Share the difference between identical and fraternal twins, for instance. If any students are twins, let them share their experiences.

5

Sunday	Monday	Tuesday	Wednesday	Thursday	Friday	Saturday

June

June Gazette

Teacher _____ Date _____

IN THE NEWS

TAKE NOTE

WHAT'S COMING UP

KID'S CORNER
Color the picture below.

Celebrate June!

Dear Family Members,
Here are a few quick-and-easy activities to help you and your child celebrate special days throughout the month of June.

June is *Fresh Fruit and Vegetable Month*

- Have your child help you make this tasty Summer Fruit Salad.
  - $\frac{1}{2}$ cup orange juice
  - $\frac{1}{4}$ cup honey
  - 1 pint strawberries, stemmed and halved
  - 1 half-pint raspberries
  - 1 half-pint blueberries
  - 2 oranges, peeled and cut into sections
  - 1 cup cantaloupe

In a medium bowl, combine orange juice and honey. Combine fruit in a large bowl. Gently toss the dressing over the fruit. Chill for one hour before serving. Makes 4 servings.

June is *Student Safety Month*

- Talk with your child about ways to be safe at school. Then, have your child make a list of all the rules and decorate it. Post the list on the refrigerator during June.

Father's Day is the third Sunday in June

- Have your child make a special picture collage for Dad of things that he likes. Look through magazines, newspapers, photographs, etc., for appropriate pictures. Glue the pictures to a small piece of poster board. Help your child wrap the gift, then surprise Dad!

June is *National Iced Tea Month*

- You and your child can cool off with this Spiced Iced Tea.
  - 3 cups boiling water
  - 4 Orange and Spice tea bags
  - 1 6-ounce can frozen lemonade concentrate, undiluted

Pour boiling water over tea bags. Cover and steep 5 minutes. Remove tea bags. Stir in lemonade. Chill for about 30 minutes. Serve in ice-filled glasses. Makes 3 servings.

National Hug Week is June 6-12

- Make a promise to your child to give him or her at least two hugs this week. Send long distance hugs by tracing, cutting out, and gluing two hands on either side of a greeting card.

June 21 is *First Day of Summer*

- Talk with your child about what he or she likes to do on a hot summer day, then take a family poll. Write down the top three choices. The next hot day when everyone is available, complete one of the activities as a family.

Read In June!

Dear Family Members,
Here are some books to share with your child to enhance the enjoyment of reading in June.

 Commotion in the Ocean by Giles Andreae
  - *Fun poems describe various sea creatures.*
  - Have your child choose a favorite animal, write a poem about it, then illustrate the animal.

 Creeps from the Deep by Leighton R. Taylor
  - *Photographs show the reader firsthand what life is like at the bottom of the ocean.*
  - Pretend you and your child are in a submarine. Take turns describing the creatures you both see on the journey.

 How to Hide an Octopus by Ruth Heller
  - *Illustrations and rhyming text inform readers about the camouflage techniques of several different sea creatures.*
  - Have your child draw and cut out a large octopus shape. Take turns hiding and finding the octopus.

 In the Swim by Douglas Florian
  - *Features short poems and watercolor paintings, each focusing on a different fresh- or saltwater creature.*
  - Make ocean animal puppets with your child by drawing and cutting out pictures of the animals. Tape the pictures to drinking straws and use them to create an underwater skit.

 My Blue Boat by Chris L. Demarest
  - *A girl takes her bath boat on a make-believe ocean voyage.*
  - Have your child "sail" a toy boat around on the floor, on a table, or in the sink or tub. Encourage him or her to tell you where the boat is sailing.

 The Magic School Bus Blows Its Top by Gail Herman
  - *Ms. Frizzle takes the class on a field trip to a newly-formed volcanic island.*
  - Provide clay and have your child use it to make a volcano like the one in the story.

 An Island Scrapbook by Virginia Wright-Frierson
  - *Drawings and notations record a mother and daughter's explorations of a North Carolina island.*
  - Take your child on a walk outside and look for natural objects in the environment. Then, have him or her draw and label the objects to create a nature scrapbook.

July

Day-by-Day Calendar

1 *International Joke Day* Have students share a "teacher-approved" joke with the class.

2 *Music for Life Week* is celebrated during the first full week in July. Share various types of music such as classical, pop, rock, etc., with the class. Make a class graph titled *Our Favorite Types of Music*.

3 *Read an Almanac Month* Place several children's almanacs in a reading center. Encourage students to read them and share the facts they learn with the class.

4 *Stephen Foster's Birthday* The songwriter was born on this day in 1826. Sing *Oh! Susanna*, one of his most popular songs, in his honor.

5 *Anti-Boredom Month* Have students brainstorm a list of things to do during this month. Then, create a bulletin board listing those activities.

6 *Beatrix Potter's Birthday* This children's author was born today in 1866. Read *Peter Rabbit* to the class. Then, see if students can remember all of the characters in the story. Help them make a list.

7 *The Adventures of Pinocchio* by Carlo Collodi was published today in 1882. Share a chapter from this book with the class.

8 The *first ice cream sundae* was *sold* on this day in 1881. Have the children make construction paper sundaes depicting their favorite flavors.

9 *National Baked Bean Month* Have students make a list of foods that go well with baked beans.

10 *It was a record 134° in Death Valley, California* on this day in 1913. Have students imagine they were in Death Valley on that day in 1913. Then, have them complete this sentence: "It was so hot you could...." Have students illustrate their sentences.

11 *E.B. White's Birthday* The famous author was born on this day in 1899. Read or watch *Charlotte's Web* in his honor.

12 The *Etch-A-Sketch®* toy *went on sale* on this day in 1960. Bring in an Etch-A-Sketch and let students examine it. Then, have them draw straight line Etch-A-Sketch illustrations using rulers and colored markers.

13 *Tennis Month* Teach students some basic tennis terms—how to keep score (love, twenty, thirty, forty, deuce, game), what it means to ace a serve, etc.

14 The *tape measure* was *patented* on this day in 1868. Bring in a tape measure and have students measure different classroom objects.

15 *Respect Canada Day* Have students research facts about Canada, such as its average temperature, size, etc., and share with the class.

16 *The District of Columbia* was *established* on this day in 1790. Provide each student with a construction paper cutout of the U.S. Have them locate Washington, D.C. on a map and place a star there.

17 *Karla Kuskin's Birthday* This children's author was born today in 1932. Share her story *The Upstairs Cat* with the class. Then, have students brainstorm a list of positive ways to solve problems.

18 *National Recreation and Parks Month* Visit a local parks and recreation facility or show pictures of a national park.

19 *Susan Montgomery Williams blew a bubble gum bubble with a 23-inch diameter* on this day in 1994. Blow up a balloon with a 23-inch diameter to show students the size of this record-breaking bubble.

20 *Edmund Hillary's Birthday* He was the first person to successfully climb Mount Everest and was born on this day in 1919. Share pictures of Mount Everest with the class.

21 The *National Women's Hall of Fame* was *founded* on this day in 1979. Have students write or tell about women they admire.

22 *Alexander Calder's Birthday* The creator of the mobile was born on this day in 1848. Have the class make mobiles by decorating sun shapes and tying them to beach pail shapes.

23 *National Hot Dog Month* Provide a hot dog lunch for students complete with chili, mustard, ketchup, cheese, etc.

24 *Amelia Earhart's Birthday* The first woman to cross the Atlantic in an airplane was born on this day in 1898. Have students make paper airplanes and see how far they can fly.

25 *Puerto Rico became a commonwealth of the United States* on this day in 1952. Enlarge the flag of Puerto Rico for students to color.

26 *Apollo 15* was *launched* on this day in 1971. The passengers stayed on the moon for almost three days. Have students make a list of things they would pack if they were visiting the moon for three days.

27 *Bugs Bunny made his debut* on this day in 1940. Have students draw cartoon rabbits and share them with the class.

28 *Bananas first arrived in the U.S.* on this date in 1871. Have students write a journal as if they were giving their first reactions to the fruit.

29 *July Belongs to Blueberries Month* Treat the class to blueberry muffins to celebrate.

30 *Henry Ford's Birthday* The inventor of the Model T car was born on this day in 1863. Have students cut out pictures of cars from the newspaper to create a car collage.

31 *National Barbecue Month* Bring in paper plates and art materials. Have students cut out construction paper shapes of their favorite barbecue dishes, such as ribs, coleslaw, etc., to glue to the paper plates. Display on a bulletin board or wall.

Sunday	Monday	Tuesday	Wednesday	Thursday	Friday	Saturday

July

July Gazette

Teacher_____ Date_____

IN THE NEWS

TAKE NOTE

WHAT'S COMING UP

KID'S CORNER

boat
pool
swim
sun
basket
picnic

p	b	o	a	t	t
s	i	i	e	e	s
w	l	c	k	b	u
i	d	s	n	d	n
m	a	h	i	i	i
b	p	o	o	l	c

Celebrate July!

Dear Family Members,
Here are a few quick-and-easy activities to help you and your child celebrate special days throughout the month of July.

July is *National Hot Dog Month*

- Ask family members what they like to eat on their hot dogs. Then, plan a hot dog dinner with your child. Help your child prepare the meal, then enjoy as a family!

July is *Blueberry Month*

- Take a trip to your local library with your child and read the book *Blueberries for Sal* by Robert McCloskey. Then, purchase some blueberries to enjoy as a snack.

July is *National Barbecue Month*

- Have a family barbecue picnic complete with traditional foods like hamburgers, watermelon, and corn on the cob. Let your child choose a special place to have the picnic.

International Joke Day is July 1

- Have each member of the family tell a favorite joke in honor of this day.

Independence Day is July 4

- Discuss fireworks safety with your child. Then, find out where the fireworks display will be in your town and view it with your child.

The first ice cream sundae was sold on July, 8, 1881

- You and your child can use this recipe to make homemade ice cream.
  - 1 cup whole milk
  - 1 cup heavy whipping cream
  - $\frac{1}{2}$ cup sugar
  - $\frac{1}{2}$ teaspoon vanilla
  - pinch of salt
  - rock salt
  - crushed ice cubes
  - 1 empty 12-ounce coffee can
  - 1 empty 39-ounce coffee can
  - masking tape

Stir the milk and cream together in a large bowl. Mix in sugar, vanilla, and salt. Fill the small coffee can about two inches from the top with the mixture. Put the lid on the can and seal the top with masking tape. Place the small can inside the large can. Sprinkle some crushed ice around the small can, then sprinkle some rock salt around it. Alternately sprinkle crushed ice and rock salt in the large can until it is full. Put the lid on the large can. Continuously roll the can back and forth on a smooth surface for 20-25 minutes. When you open the can, you should have ice cream!

Read In July!

Dear Family Members,
Here are some books to share with your child to enhance the enjoyment of reading in July.

 One Hundred Hungry Ants by Elinor J. Pinczes
- *When one hundred hungry ants decide to march toward a picnic, they divide into different groups to help them get there faster.*
- After reading the story, ask your child to name some of the animals in the story and the picnic foods they took.

 Bailey Goes Camping by Kevin Henkes
- *When Bailey cannot go on a camping trip because he is too young, his mother shows him how to camp where he is.*
- Drape blankets or sheets over a table to create an indoor tent and pretend to camp out with your child.

 The Bears' Picnic by Stan and Jan Berenstain
- *The Berenstain Bears search and search for just the right picnic place.*
- Spread a large blanket on the floor and have an indoor picnic with your child.

 Arthur Goes to Camp by Marc T. Brown
- *Arthur the aardvark is homesick and ready to escape from camp until something unexpected happens to change his mind.*
- Ask your child to describe what he or she would do if he or she were the main character in the story.

 Once Upon a Picnic by John Prater
- *A little boy on a picnic notices different storybook characters all around him.*
- Ask your child to name the storybook characters that appear in the book.

 Watermelon Day by Kathi Appelt
- *Jesse waits patiently all summer for her watermelon to grow and is excited when it is finally ripe and ready to eat.*
- Help your child plant and care for a watermelon seed.

Hurray for the Fourth of July by Wendy Watson
- *Cheerful text and engaging illustrations take the reader through a small town Independence Day parade, picnic, and fireworks display.*
- Provide a shoebox along with red, white, and blue paper. Have your child make a miniature Independence Day float using the supplies.

YOU DID IT!

Name _____

For _____

_____

Signed _____

Date _____

Thanks For Your Helping Hand!

Name _____

For _____

_____

Signed _____

Date _____

BRILLIANT WORK!

✓+ Super! Job!

Name _____

Signed _____

Date _____

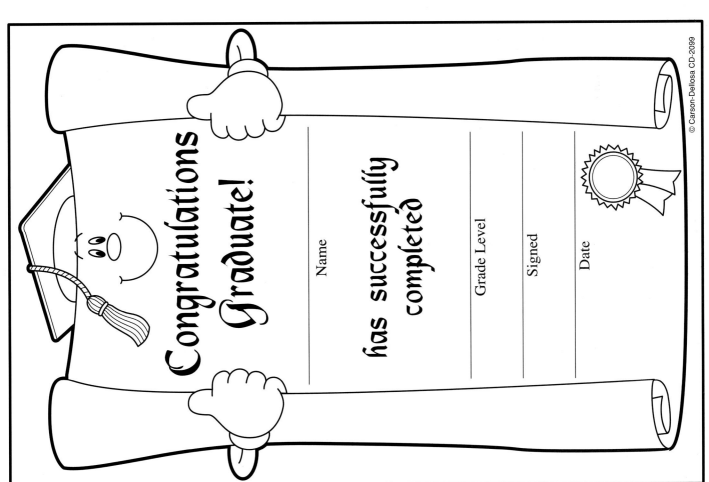

Congratulations Graduate!

Name _____

has successfully completed

Grade Level _____

Signed _____

Date _____

JUNE
Writing Activities

What's a child's favorite month? Let's see... fireflies, campfires, watermelon, water slides, cool treats, and long days... it has to be June! Focus writing exercises this month on these and other favorite June activities, such as year-end projects and helping students say good-bye for the summer!

Word Bank Words

boat	seashell	swim
sand	shark	beach
castle	dolphin	sail
island	water	float
ocean	fish	summer

Viva Ice Cream!

The ice cream soda was invented in June of 1874—and long may it fizz! Jumble up the steps for making the perfect ice cream soda and write them on a chart. Have children list the steps in the proper order and then follow them to make their own ice cream sodas!

Wash and dry hands.
Place a clean tall glass on the table.
Open the vanilla ice cream.
Spoon one scoop of vanilla ice cream.
Place a scoop of vanilla ice cream in the glass.
Open the soda.
Pour the soda slowly over the ice cream.
Put a straw and a spoon in the glass.
Put away the "melting" ice cream.
Close the "going flat" soda.
Drink the soda politely, please...no slurping!

Thanks for the Memories!

Cherish your memories! Begin a tradition of having your students create a class memory book at the end of each school year. Have each child draw a picture of his favorite memory of the year and caption it with a few sentences about the event. Put the book together by punching holes and lacing with yarn. Use poster board to create a cover with the title *Mrs. _____'s Class Memories of 20__ – 20__*. Include a page with names of the contributors and a class picture, if possible. In future years, children can return to your room to look at the book, and current students can enjoy looking at the memory books from previous classes.

I liked reading time the best.

I remember playing kickball. It was fun.

See You Next Year

Goodbye and have a great summer! Let each student draw another child's name out of a hat and write that child a farewell letter. Students can include a memory of that particular student and relate their own plans for the summer.

Diamanté Poems-They're Not That Hard!

Honor the month of June! Ask students to think of a word associated with June. Instruct them to follow the format of the sample poem and to follow the directions (below) for each line.

Directions:

1st line: One word title.
2nd line: Two adjectives describing the title.
3rd line: Three verbs ending in *-ing* that tell what the word in the title does.
4th line: Four nouns: the first two should be about the title, the second two about the opposite word on the 7th line. (Finish the poem, then write these two words last.)
5th line: Three verbs ending in *-ing* that tell what the opposite word does.
6th line: Two adjectives describing the opposite word.
7th line: One word that is the opposite of the title.

Sun
yellow, hot
rising, shining, setting
light, heat, craters, shadows
changing, glowing, grinning
cool, white
Moon

Ocean Myths

The ocean has always been the inspiration for many stories, myths, legends, and tall tales. Read a story of this type aloud to the class, such as *Seven Chinese Brothers* or *The Little Mermaid*. Then, have students write stories explaining why there are waves in the ocean.

Sense-ational Summer!

Help students make a list of the sights and sounds, the tastes and smells of summer! Write the topics on the board and see how many things they can name. For example: smells—charcoal grills, cut grass; sounds—frogs, crickets; tastes—lemonade, peaches; sights—fireflies, flowers, etc.

19

JULY
Writing Activities

The firecrackers, lush gardens, and heat of July can make it one of the most intense months of the year. Challenge students not to hold back, but to make their writing as exuberant as the month itself!

Word Bank Words

picnic	sandwich
camp	basket
watermelon	lemonade
fireworks	grass
ice cream	planet
parade	star
tent	space

Word Maps

Point students in the right direction! Have students make word maps for their spelling words. To make a map, write the word in a circle in the middle of the paper. Draw one line extending from the center circle and write the definition in a circle. Draw a second line and circle, then write a sentence using the word. Add more circles for the number of syllables, antonyms, synonyms, or word endings. Staple the pages together and have students use them as study guides.

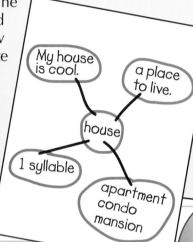

Spark the Imagination!

Use these story starters to encourage students' journal writing about July. Starters can include,

Our boat landed on a deserted island, and the first thing we did was...

On our summer trip we hiked for miles and finally found...

When the July heat gets to me, my favorite way to cool off is...

Fantastic Fireworks

Pop! Pow! Bang! Have students write descriptions of how fireworks look and sound to someone who has never seen or heard them before. Have them use similes and onomatopoeia in their descriptions, such as *Firecrackers go POP!* and *sound as loud as thunder.*

POP! BANG! BOOM! POW!

1-2-3-4-Cinquain!

Hooray for July! Let students write cinquain poems to honor favorite July activities. Cinquains are unrhymed, five-lined poems that can be as varied as a poet's imagination. Instruct children to choose one-word topics and to follow the instructions and pattern. They do not have to follow the pattern exactly, but poems must have five lines.

The first line is one word and acts as the title.
Line 2 has two words that describe the first word.
Line 3 has three words that express action.
Line 4 has four words that express feeling or emotion.
Line 5 has one word, a synonym for the first word.

Sparklers
Bright, colorful
Making lighted circles
I'm happy it's summer!
Fireworks

Message in a Bottle

SOS! Have students imagine they are stranded on a desert island. Have them write letters they would put into bottles explaining life on the island and telling about how they want to be rescued. Secure the letters with rubber bands and put them in 20-ounce plastic bottles. Place the bottles at a reading center for students to enjoy during free time.

"Let's go Camping!" she exclaimed.

Show students how to add interest to their stories. Have students write exciting, conversation-based stories about pretend camping trips. Tell them that when characters in their stories speak, they can only use new and different words in place of *said* to make the dialogue more colorful and descriptive. Brainstorm a class list of synonyms for *said*, such as *asked, called, stuttered, begged, cried, whispered*, etc. Post the list for students to refer to for future writing and editing projects.

On the Ocean Floor

Take students under the sea! Have students pretend they are on a submarine trip. Let them write about what they see around them. Instruct students to illustrate their submarines and some of the sights in their writings.

21

Bulletin Board Ideas

Use this bulletin board as a guide for locating all the unusual sea creatures in the *Into the Sea* chapter (pages 28-39). Divide a bulletin board into three horizontal sections. Cover the top with light blue paper, the middle with dark blue paper, and the bottom with dark purple or black paper. Display a large sun over the board. Label the top section *Sunlight Zone*, the middle section *Twilight Zone*, and the bottom section *Midnight Zone*, to represent the sunlight zones of the ocean. Explain to students that many sea animals live in the Sunlight Zone where food is most plentiful. At the bottom of the ocean, there is less light and food. Display the *Into the Sea* chapter (pages 28-39) projects in the appropriate zones on the bulletin board.

Fish for fun with this bulletin board idea while your students explore the *Into the Sea* unit (pages 28-39). Cover a bulletin board with blue paper to represent the ocean. Color and cut out fish patterns (page 39). Cut out free-form coral, seaweed, and rocks from construction paper and fasten them to the bulletin board. Then, hide the fish on the board peeking out from behind ocean objects of the same colors, so that the fish are camouflaged. Count the number of fish on the board and write the question *Can you find ___ fish?*, filling in the blank with the correct number. Challenge students to find all of the hidden fish on the display.

22

Accent "treasured" work with student-made treasure chests. Cover a board with blue paper to represent the ocean, and attach a large, brown, construction paper island to the bottom. Enlarge, color, and post the palm tree pattern (page 47) on the island. Give each child a treasure chest pattern (page 47) to personalize with her name. Then, let students color their chests and "fill" them with plastic gems, sequins, and glitter. Use the sparkling treasure chests to accent student work during the *A Trip to the Islands* chapter (pages 40-47).

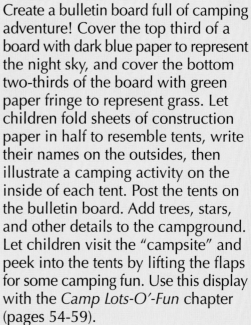

Create a bulletin board full of camping adventure! Cover the top third of a board with dark blue paper to represent the night sky, and cover the bottom two-thirds of the board with green paper fringe to represent grass. Let children fold sheets of construction paper in half to resemble tents, write their names on the outsides, then illustrate a camping activity on the inside of each tent. Post the tents on the bulletin board. Add trees, stars, and other details to the campground. Let children visit the "campsite" and peek into the tents by lifting the flaps for some camping fun. Use this display with the *Camp Lots-O'-Fun* chapter (pages 54-59).

23

Set sail on a high seas adventure during the *Ships Ahoy!* chapter (pages 48-53) with student-made "sailing tales." Decorate a bulletin board with an ocean scene. Cut lined paper into triangle shapes for sails, then cut construction paper boat shapes. On the lined paper, have students write imaginative stories about sailing adventures. If the stories are long, staple additional triangle-shaped pages behind the sails for children to use. Students can decorate their boats and add their names, then post them on the high seas bulletin board.

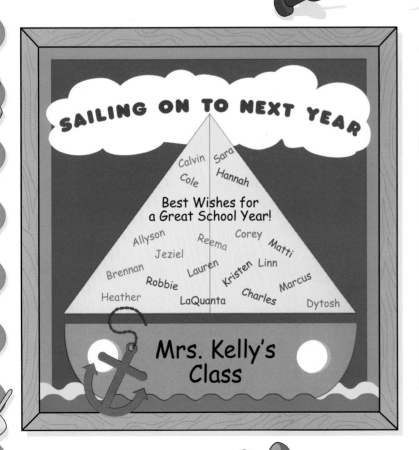

Say "Bon Voyage" to your class and wish them smooth sailing into the next school year. Decorate a bulletin board with an ocean scene. Cut out a sail and a boat shape from butcher paper. Post the sail and boat on the board. Add an anchor and portholes to the side of the boat for decoration. Then, write the names of your students along with best wishes for the next school year on the sail. Use this display with either the *Ships Ahoy!* chapter (pages 48-53) or the *Graduation* chapter (pages 68-69).

IT'S GRADUATION TIME!

Isaiah Russell Pamela Wayne Johnette

Zach Lashonda Aimee Todd

Fred Chelsea Matthew Hank Tara

Promote smiles at graduation time with this enthusiastic display. Cover a bulletin board in your school's colors. Make a graduation cap from poster board and attach it to the bulletin board. Attach a tassel to the cap. On light-colored sheets of paper, write a graduation wish from you for each child. Write each child's name on the paper, then roll up the paper to resemble a scroll and tie the scroll with ribbon. Fasten each scroll to the bulletin board. On the last day of school or during the *Graduation: A Stepping Stone* chapter (pages 68-69), present each child with a special scrolled message.

Create a sweet incentive using ice cream cone and scoop patterns (page 73). Give each child a cone pattern to label with his name. Post the cones on the bulletin board. Duplicate several ice cream scoops in different colors and place them in plastic sandwich bags attached to the board. When a student demonstrates good behavior, put a scoop of ice cream on his cone. Reward students with ice cream treats when their cones have a predetermined number of scoops. This display makes a nice companion to the *We All Scream for Ice Cream!* chapter (pages 70-73).

25

LET FREEDOM RING!

Sara · Ben · KENDRA · QUINCY · TAYLOR

Celebrate freedom along with the *Happy Birthday USA* chapter (pages 74-81), using the bell patterns (page 81). Have students decorate bottom bell patterns with red, white, and blue crayons. On another set of bottom bell patterns, have students write a few examples of things they are free to do. Fasten each set of bottom bell patterns together with a brad, making sure the pattern with student writing is "ringing" out from underneath the decorated pattern. Post the bells on a bulletin board covered with shiny red or black paper and add glitter glue fireworks.

MR. REILLY'S CLASS HAS THE RIPE STUFF

Scott · Jenny · Jacob · Katie · Jared · Eric · Lionel · Alain · Betsy · Penny · Hank · Rick · Allison

Let your students plant the seeds of knowledge they received in class. Let each child color and cut out an enlarged watermelon slice pattern (page 85). Write children's names on the melon parts and glue on real watermelon seeds. On the rind, each child should write something she learned in class. Watch the knowledge grow! Display this board with the *On a Picnic* chapter (pages 82-85).

These picnic baskets hold more than food! As you share *On a Picnic* chapter (pages 82-85) activities with your class, create an interactive math display with picnic-themed word problems. Decorate a bulletin board with green paper on the bottom to represent grass and blue paper on top to represent sky. Copy several basket patterns (page 85) on construction paper. Cut out squares of white paper and color the edges to resemble sandwiches. On each sandwich, write story problems about picnic basket items. Staple the edges of the baskets to the bulletin board, leaving open pockets at the top. Place story problem sandwiches in each pocket for students to remove and solve.

While leading your students on out-of-this-world adventures during the *Blast Off for Learning* chapter (pages 86-92), have students stretch their imaginations by pretending to be space travelers gathering scientific facts from outer space. Let each student draw a portrait of herself as an astronaut, complete with space suit and helmet. Let the class research space facts and record the facts in speech balloons. Post the speech balloons beside the astronauts. Encourage children to read the board to learn more about space.

INTO THE SEA

Budding marine biologists can get their feet wet with this fun, informative unit about mysterious, ocean-dwelling creatures.

Did You Know?

- Many sea creatures, including the octopus, crab, and starfish, can grow new legs if they are damaged or lost.
- Many fish have dark-colored backs and glow-in-the-dark spots on their bellies so that they are camouflaged to fish looking up at them into lighter water above, or down at them through darker water below.
- Sharks are vertebrates, but do not have any bones! Their skeletons are made from cartilage, the same material that forms human ears and noses.

Literature Selections

Commotion in the Ocean by Giles Andreae: Little Tiger Press, 1998. (Picture book, 32 pg.) Fun poems describing various sea creatures.

Creeps from the Deep: Life in the Deep Sea by Leighton R. Taylor: Chronicle Books, 1997. (Picture book, 48 pg.) Photos show the reader firsthand what life is like at the bottom of the ocean.

How to Hide an Octopus by Ruth Heller: Grosset/Putnam, 1992. (Picture book, 32 pg.) Describes the different camouflage techniques of several sea creatures.

Seashells, Crabs, and Sea Stars by Christiane Kump Tibbitts: Northwood Press, 1999. (Reference book, 48 pg.) Examines seashells, crabs, sea stars, sand dollars, and more.

Be a "Grouper"

A *grouper* is a fish, but a grouper is also a student who can "group" or classify sea animals! Challenge pairs of students to think of as many sea creatures as they can. Then, ask the pairs to list ways to classify sea creatures. Explain that there are so many ways to classify sea animals that scientists have to agree on one classification system. This system, or *taxonomy*, is based mostly on body parts and functionality, such as whether an animal has a backbone, lays eggs, or has a hard shell. Enlarge a different sea animal pattern (pages 37-39) for each group listed below. Describe each category (sea mammal, fish, etc.) and write it on a corresponding pattern. Then, let children list the names of the creatures on separate pieces of paper and attach them under the correct headings.

FISH

Spiny-Skinned Sea Animals

fish = shark (page 37), seahorse, angelfish
sea mammals = dolphin (page 37), whale
animals in seashells = oyster (page 39), clam
joint-legged sea animals = crab (page 38), lobster, shrimp
sea jellies = jellyfish (page 38), sea anemone
spiny-skinned sea animals = starfish (page 38), sea urchin, sand dollar (page 37)

Scale a Fish

Make quite a catch with these colorful paper fish. Provide shiny wrapping paper, heavy-duty aluminum foil, a hole punch, and a large bowl. Punch holes in the wrapping paper and foil over the opening of the bowl. Let students dot fish patterns (page 39) with glue and sprinkle the patterns with the paper punches, creating tiny, shiny scales. Show off your school of fish by hanging them on a bulletin board covered with blue paper or from the ceiling.

Sink or Swim

What do a fish and a submarine have in common? They can both sink or float by taking air in or pushing it out! Submarines have special tanks that fill with water when the sub needs to dive deep into the water, and then fill with air (which is lighter than water) when the sub needs to rise toward the surface. Fish have similar "tanks," called *swim bladders*, which let air in and out to help them rise and sink in the water. For the class, provide a clear container almost full of water, two balloons, and two marbles. Push a marble into the neck of each balloon. Blow air into one balloon and tie it at the neck. Tie the empty balloon close to the marble. What will happen when the balloons are submerged? Put both balloons in the water and record any observations. Why does the balloon with air float and the balloon without air sink? Which balloon represents a fish's swim bladder when it is deep in the water, and which represents a swim bladder when it is close to the surface?

Light Up My Life

Children will be all aglow when they create their own glow-in-the-dark deep sea creatures. Some sea creatures, such as the angler fish, some sea cucumbers, and the hatchet fish, live too deep in the ocean for natural light to reach them. These creatures have special cells in certain parts of their bodies that create their own light! This light is called *bioluminescence*. Show pictures of these fish and let students create brand new deep sea creatures with unique features, using glow-in-the-dark paint to add details. When the bioluminescent creatures are complete, darken the room and "swim" the creatures through the dark.

A Fish-Eat-Fish World

What would a squid order for dinner? A food chain mobile can help your students find out. Explain that the food chain has *consumers* and *producers*. Producers make their own food, usually from the sun's energy, while consumers eat either producers or other consumers. Most sea life chains start with producers called *phytoplankton*, and often the first consumers in the food chain are tiny animals called *zooplankton*. Ask each student to choose a sea creature and research what it eats, tracing its place on the food chain back to phytoplankton and the sun. To make a mobile, have each student color and cut out a sun, the animals in the chain, and the original animal. Punch holes in the bottoms and tops of the creatures and string them together in order from the sun to the chosen animal. Hang the mobiles around the room, and challenge children to find their creatures in other students' food chains.

Shark! (or is it a Dolphin?)

From the surface, sharks and dolphins are easily mistaken for each other because both have dorsal fins that stick out of the water. Dolphins are sea mammals called *cetaceans* that must come to the surface to breathe air. Sharks are fish with gills and must get oxygen from the water. The easiest way to tell dolphins from sharks is by looking at their tails. Sea mammal tails are horizontal (flat) and move up and down, while fish tails are vertical and move from side to side. Follow the steps below to make dioramas showing the differences between the two types of tails. Use lidless shoe boxes, and the dolphin, shark, and tail patterns (page 37).

1. Cut out one long side of the box. Turn the box upside down (the bottom of the box is the top of this project) and cover the top with blue paper. Cut two slits through the box top and the paper. Write *Shark or Dolphin?* on the top of the box. Decorate the inside of the box to look like an underwater scene.

2. Color and cut out the patterns. Cut a slit in the back of the dolphin and in the tail pattern, then fit them together so that the dolphin's tail is horizontal.

3. Place the dolphin and shark inside the box, and stick the dorsal fin of each pattern through one slit in the top of the box, so that only the dorsal fins show through. Cover the front of the diorama with clear plastic, and write a brief explanation of the differences between sharks and dolphins on a strip of paper. Glue the strip of paper across the front of the diorama.

Dolphins and sharks both have dorsal fins that can be seen above the water, but you can tell the difference between them by looking at their tail fins. A dolphin is a mammal. Its tail fin is horizontal. A shark is a fish. Its tail fin is vertical.

Full of Beans

A starfish is neither a star nor a fish! It is an *echinoderm*, which means *spiny-skinned*. Create starfish beanbags with your students and play a round of *Tidepool Toss* (see below). Trace and cut out two enlarged starfish patterns (page 38) onto a piece of fabric. Place one pattern face down on a table and outline it with fabric glue, leaving a 1/2" space free of glue. Press the other pattern on top of the glue, matching the edges. Fill the starfish with beans, then glue the remaining edge closed, and play the game! To make textured, "prickly" starfish, color a piece of sandpaper with crayons, then place one fabric starfish on top. Press with a hot iron to transfer the pattern to the fabric.

Tidepool Toss

This game is sure to make a big splash! Sea urchins, mussels, crabs, anemones, and starfish live in shallow pools of water, called tidepools, that form on rocks or sand when the tide is out. The shallow pools get a lot of sunlight, which gives energy to various algae and seaweeds. These plants feed the plant eaters in the tidepools, which in turn feed meat eaters like crabs and starfish. Place a large sheet of butcher paper on the floor and decorate it like a tidepool. Have students stand back from the paper and try to "feed" their beanbag starfish by tossing them onto other animals in the tidepool. Award 1 point for landing on an animal, no points for landing anywhere else in the tidepool, and subtract 2 points for landing outside of the tidepool (since starfish can die outside of a tidepool). Reward the players with starfruit, star-shaped cookies, or stickers.

A Pearl of a Poem

Most seashells once belonged to *mollusks*; soft, boneless animals with hard shells to protect them. The oyster has two shells that are jointed by a hinge and held together by a powerful muscle. The inside of an oyster shell is lined with a shiny substance called *mother-of-pearl*. If an irritating grain of sand gets inside the oyster shell, the oyster covers the sand with layers of mother-of-pearl to smooth it out. Over time, the layers create a round, smooth object inside the oyster: a pearl! Have students write poems about how sand turns into pearls. Trace an oyster pattern (page 39) on a piece of gray paper, then cut it out (do not cut through the hinge in the center). Students can rewrite their poems on the fronts of the shell patterns. Line the insides of the oysters with clear glue and iridescent cellophane wrapping paper to be the mother-of-pearl. Glue an oval of pink or gray paper to the cellophane to represent the oyster, then glue a plastic pearl to each. Finally, decorate a box to look like a bed, and place the oysters in their oyster bed for a little "bedtime" reading!

I am an oyster
As you can see.
I am as happy as I can be.
But if some sand gets in my shell
I do not like it very well.
I will cover it and make it round.
So when I am opened...

A pearl is found!

31

I See Seashells!

Dig in! Set up a large box lined with a plastic garbage bag, and fill it with sand. Hide seashells (use laminated pictures of shells if real ones are not available) in the sand. Provide plastic shovels, sifters, buckets, and books about seashells. As children dig up shells, have them identify the shells using the books, then record their findings.

An Octopus of Many Colors

The octopus is famous for having many legs, but it can also have many colors. The octopus changes colors to blend in with its surroundings or to scare away predators. If threatened, it can also squirt dark ink into the water, then escape behind the cloud of ink. Let students make hidden octopus books from four copies of the octopus pattern, (page 37), two sheets of white paper, and one sheet of construction paper. Fold the papers in half to make a book, with the construction paper as a cover, and staple the folded edge. On each page, color and label an underwater scene with a different color scheme. For example, one page could feature green and brown seaweed, while another could show the blue ocean. Color the octopus patterns to match the different color schemes on the pages, then glue the patterns onto the pages. On the last page, color the remaining octopus any color, glue it to the page, then spread black paint over the pattern, so that it is hiding behind the cloud of ink. Have students trade books and take turns finding each others' octopi.

Sand $$$$

What can you buy with a sand dollar? Challenge students to imagine what they think a sand dollar might buy, then write word problems featuring sand dollars. For example: *Juan wanted some sand for his sand box and a new pail and shovel. Sand costs 5 sand dollars a pound, pails cost 2 sand dollars, and shovels cost 1 sand dollar. How many sand dollars will Juan need for a pail, a shovel, and 2 pounds of sand?* When the word problems are complete, cut out sand dollar patterns (page 37) and let students use them as manipulatives to solve the math problems.

Let's Be Crabby!

Imagine having crab claws instead of hands! Crabs and lobsters belong to the *crustacean* group. Crustaceans have jointed legs, hard shells, and usually two pincer claws. Crabs use their claws to pick up objects and help them eat. Bring in pictures of crabs with claws and look for similarities and differences between claws and hands. Then, let students use masking tape to tape together the four fingers of each hand, then try to perform some everyday tasks, such as eating, buttoning buttons, tying shoes, etc., with crab claws. How is it different from having hands? How would a crab's life be different if it had fingers? Which would your students rather have, claws or fingers?

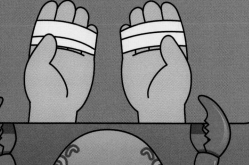

Jiggling Jellyfish

Jellyfish, like starfish, are not really fish! These invertebrates, which belong to a group of sea creatures called *sea jellies*, have no backbones, gills, hearts, or brains! They do have long, stinging tentacles that they use to catch food. Provide clear, empty produce bags. Blow some air into a bag, twist the bag closed, and then tie a knot in the bag. For tentacles, let children tape lengths of pink, purple, and clear ribbon around the knot. Hang the "jellyfish" around the room.

All PUFFED Up

Don't make this fish angry! When the porcupine fish senses danger, it fills its stomach with water or air and puffs up like a balloon. The porcupine fish has spikes all over its body, which stick out when it is puffed up, warning other fish to stay away. When the danger passes, the porcupine fish shrinks to normal size and the spikes lay flat along its body. To make a spiked porcupine fish, let each child draw a fish face on the bottom of a paper lunch bag, then wrap a rubber band around the open end. Cut out construction paper fins and 1½" long triangles for spikes. Fold a small tab at the edge of each fin and each triangle. Glue the tabs of the fins to the sides of the bag. Then, glue the spikes to the "body" of the fish. Smooth the spikes so that they lie flat against the bag. Then, blow into the bag and puff it up so that the spikes stick out. To return the fish to normal, push the air out of the bag and smooth down the spikes.

33

Sea Horse Pencil Pal

You can't ride this horse, because it's only 4" tall! The sea horse is a unique fish, which swims vertically with its head up. When a sea horse stops to eat or rest, it grabs onto coral or seaweed with its tail. Make a fuzzy sea horse pencil pal and wrap it around some "pencil coral."

1. Cut off the first "bump" of a thick-and-thin pipe cleaner (available at craft stores).
2. Trim the fuzzy part from the bottom of the pipe cleaner.
3. Bend the top of the pipe cleaner to make the mouth. Curve the top of the cleaner over to make the head and curve the thick section in slightly to make the stomach.
4. To complete the sea horse, glue a wiggly eye on either side of the sea horse's head, and glue a small, fan-shaped, paper dorsal fin to the back of the pipe cleaner. Curl the sea horse's tail around a pencil.

Sharks and Fishes

It's eat or be eaten in this exciting predator and prey game! Divide a large play area into three sections. Label the two outer sections *coral* and *seaweed*, and the center section *open water*. Choose a student to be the "shark." All of the other players are fish. The fish must "swim" from the safe hiding area of the coral to the safe hiding area of the seaweed without getting caught by the shark. The shark cannot go into the coral or seaweed, but he must catch as many fish as possible in the open water, and like real sharks, he must keep swimming so that he doesn't die. As the shark catches (tags) the fish, they must sit outside of the playing area. The last fish left is the shark in the next round. Students may discover what fish already know—there's safety in numbers!

Sea Urchin Snack

Many animals, such as lobsters and sea otters, dine on the spiny sea urchin despite its menacing appearance. Make a tasty and not-so-threatening sea urchin snack, starting with cupcakes frosted with chocolate frosting. Push stick pretzels into the top of the cupcake so that they poke out in all directions. For extra fun, have children try to eat their sea urchins with lobster claw hands (see *Let's Be Crabby,* page 33).

34

Scuba Story

After learning about all of the different creatures that live in the sea, close your eyes and imagine what you would see if you were scuba diving. Scuba is an acronym which means *Self-Contained Underwater Breathing Apparatus*. Let each child trace a scuba mask pattern (page 39) twice onto poster board and then cut out a "viewing area" in the center of one copy. Cover the hole with plastic wrap and secure it with tape. Then, trace the pattern onto white paper five times, and cut out the patterns to make pages of a book. Draw an underwater scene on each page, and write one letter from the word *scuba* at the top. Draw animals, plants, and objects on each page that begin with or contain the corresponding letter from the word *scuba*. Tape the two poster board scuba masks together along the left edge, leaving the open-faced mask pattern on top. Place the inside pages together on top of the bottom mask and staple it on the right side.

Delicious Ocean Food

Enjoy this tasty snack as you complete ocean animals activities in this unit. Use a star- or fish-shaped cookie cutter to cut shapes from slices of bread. Spread each slice with cream cheese or peanut butter. Sprinkle a small amount of puffed rice cereal over each starfish to make a textured surface. Eat the crunchy sandwiches open-faced.

35

Fishing For Words

Name _____

Circle the words from the word list in the puzzle below. Words may be found horizontally, vertically, or diagonally.

```
L O B S T E R H H
S D F I S H S C
Q T O D X I A R
U F Q L F M B A
I N T R P X K B
D G A A F H C G
L T F U G A I T
S S H A R K Q N
```

CRAB   DOLPHIN   FISH   LOBSTER

SHARK   SQUID   STARFISH

sand dollar

octopus

shark

dolphin

dolphin tail

COPY and CUT

37

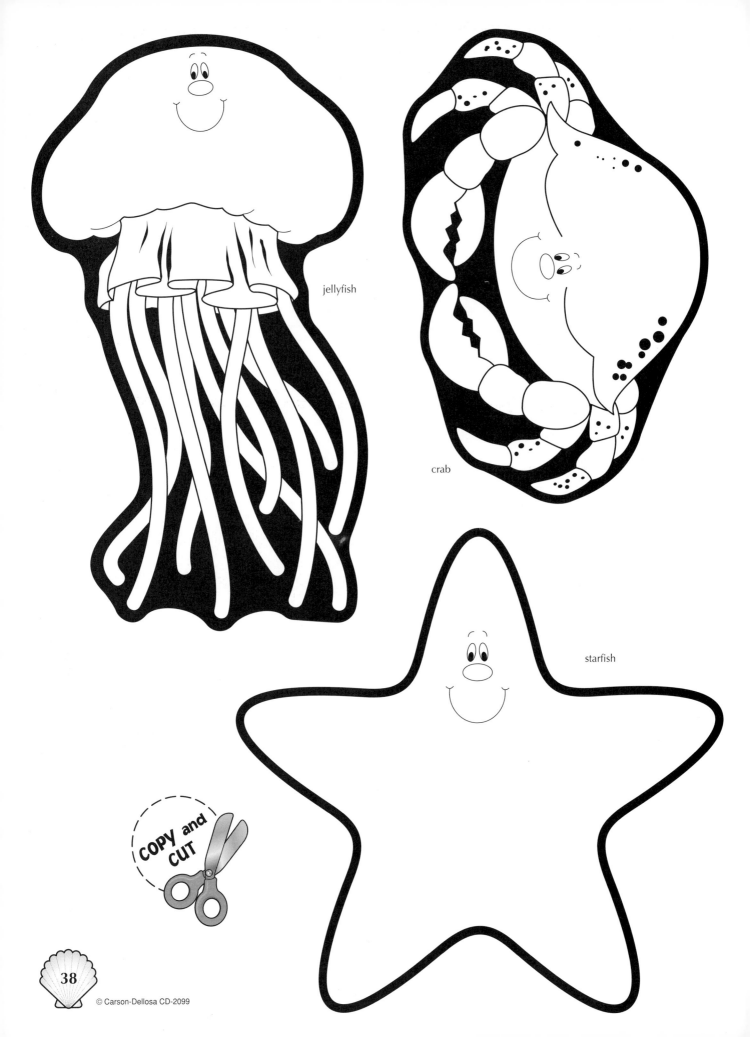

jellyfish

crab

starfish

COPY and CUT

38

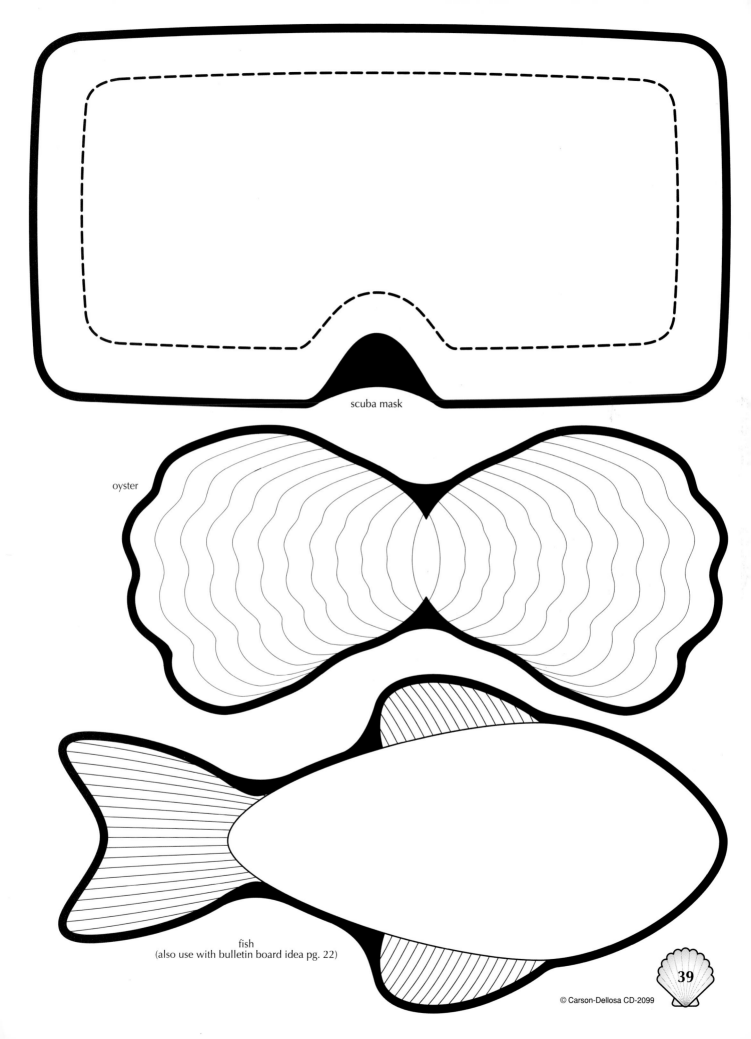

scuba mask

oyster

fish
(also use with bulletin board idea pg. 22)

39

A TRIP TO THE

There's more to islands than beaches and palm trees! An island is a land mass that is completely surrounded by water and is smaller than a continent. Islands form in one of four ways: land separates from a continent, volcanoes erupt under the ocean, sediment deposits near a shore, or coral formations rise above sea level. In this unit, explore an example of each type, and don't forget to have some island fun!

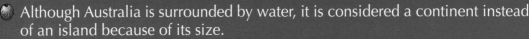

DID YOU KNOW?

- Although Australia is surrounded by water, it is considered a continent instead of an island because of its size.
- Some islands have never been inhabited by humans, while others, such as Hong Kong and Manhattan, have highly populated cities.
- Islands can sometimes appear or disappear overnight because of volcanic activity, sinking of the ocean floor, and the rise and fall of sea level.

LITERATURE SELECTIONS

Coral Reef (Watch it Grow) by Kate Scarborough: Time Life, 1997. (Reference book, 24 pg.) Reference book about the development of a coral reef.

Habitats: Islands by Julia Waterlow: Thomson Learning, 1995. (Picture book, 48 pg.) Full of facts and pictures of islands.

An Island Scrapbook: Dawn to Dusk on a Barrier Island by Virginia Wright-Frierson: Simon & Schuster, 1998. (Picture book, 40 pg.) Drawings and notations record a mother and daughter's explorations of a North Carolina island.

The Magic Schoolbus Blows its Top by Joanna Cole: Scholastic, 1996. (Picture book, 32 pg.) Ms. Frizzle takes the class on a field trip to a newly formed volcanic island.

ANY PORT IN A STORM

Get your class into an island frame of mind! First, turn out the lights and play a tape of storm or ocean sounds while pretending to be on a ship during a storm. Turn on the lights and say "We're shipwrecked on a deserted island!" Make small groups responsible for providing a necessity for the whole class, such as shelter, food, clean water, etc. List all the resources available on the island, such as coconut trees, seashells, wood from the wrecked boat, etc., and challenge groups to creatively use their resources to complete their assignments.

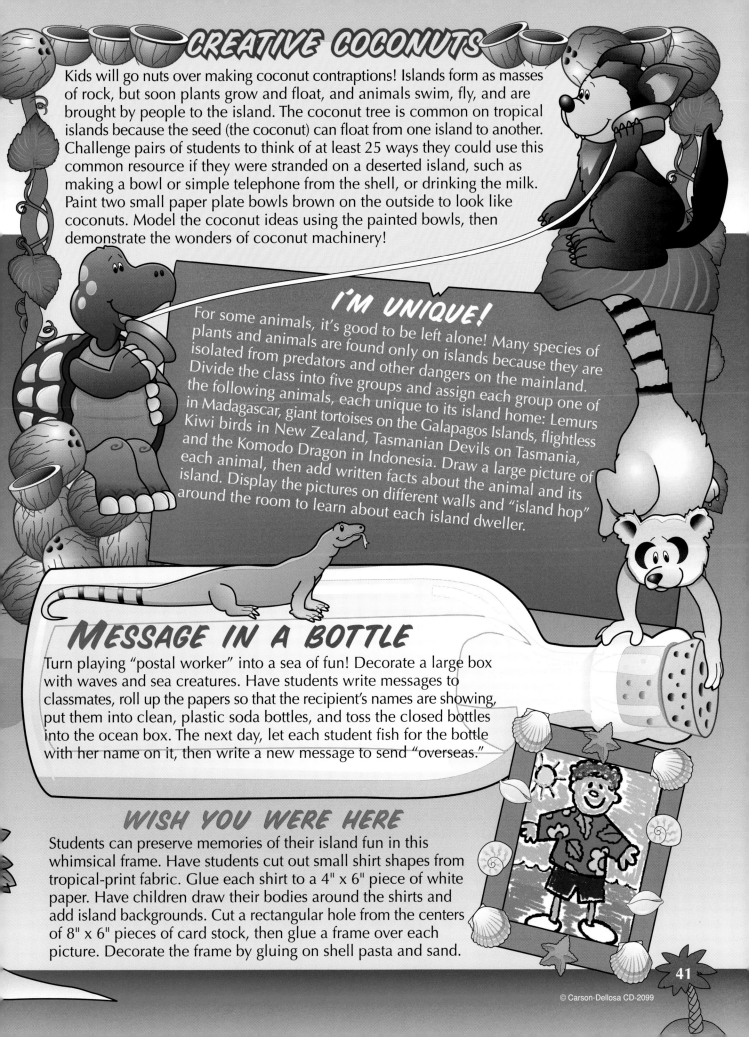

CREATIVE COCONUTS

Kids will go nuts over making coconut contraptions! Islands form as masses of rock, but soon plants grow and float, and animals swim, fly, and are brought by people to the island. The coconut tree is common on tropical islands because the seed (the coconut) can float from one island to another. Challenge pairs of students to think of at least 25 ways they could use this common resource if they were stranded on a deserted island, such as making a bowl or simple telephone from the shell, or drinking the milk. Paint two small paper plate bowls brown on the outside to look like coconuts. Model the coconut ideas using the painted bowls, then demonstrate the wonders of coconut machinery!

I'M UNIQUE!

For some animals, it's good to be left alone! Many species of plants and animals are found only on islands because they are isolated from predators and other dangers on the mainland. Divide the class into five groups and assign each group one of the following animals, each unique to its island home: Lemurs in Madagascar, giant tortoises on the Galapagos Islands, flightless Kiwi birds in New Zealand, Tasmanian Devils on Tasmania, and the Komodo Dragon in Indonesia. Draw a large picture of each animal, then add written facts about the animal and its island. Display the pictures on different walls and "island hop" around the room to learn about each island dweller.

MESSAGE IN A BOTTLE

Turn playing "postal worker" into a sea of fun! Decorate a large box with waves and sea creatures. Have students write messages to classmates, roll up the papers so that the recipient's names are showing, put them into clean, plastic soda bottles, and toss the closed bottles into the ocean box. The next day, let each student fish for the bottle with her name on it, then write a new message to send "overseas."

WISH YOU WERE HERE

Students can preserve memories of their island fun in this whimsical frame. Have students cut out small shirt shapes from tropical-print fabric. Glue each shirt to a 4" x 6" piece of white paper. Have children draw their bodies around the shirts and add island backgrounds. Cut a rectangular hole from the centers of 8" x 6" pieces of card stock, then glue a frame over each picture. Decorate the frame by gluing on shell pasta and sand.

GREENLAND A CONTINENTAL ISLAND

DID YOU KNOW?

- Continental islands form when erosion or flooding separates tracts of land, or by the movement of the Earth's plates. *Plate tectonics* is a scientific theory claiming that the outer layer of the Earth is made of about 30 plates that move over a hot layer of rock.
- Greenland is the largest island in the world, but most of the island lies within the Arctic Circle and is covered with ice.
- Greenland has been the home of Vikings originally from Scandinavia, other Europeans, and Inuits, as well as polar bears, walruses, and reindeer.

A PUZZLE OF CONTINENTAL PROPORTIONS

The Earth will move when students see how continental islands, such as Greenland, are formed. Scientists believe that the Earth's continents used to be one large land mass. This land mass is called *Pangea*, which means *all the world*. Because of plate tectonics, the land broke apart and the pieces drifted to their present locations. Let students use the Pangea puzzle (page 46) to make Pangea models. Cut along the lines of the puzzle to separate the pieces, arrange the pieces to form Pangea, then make them drift apart and arrange them to look as they do today. Where do students think the pieces of land will move in the future?

GLITTERING GLACIERS

THULE
ARCTIC OCEAN
GODTHAAB

Geography can be "cool" if you're learning about glaciers! Glaciers are thick layers of ice, formed from compacted snow, that cover the land. Use a map to show students that most of Greenland is covered by a glacier, and only the edges of the shoreline are inhabitable by humans. Demonstrate the inhabitable area on Greenland with individual maps. Glue a pattern of Greenland (page 46) to a blue sheet of paper, then color the edges green. Cover the glaciated part of the island with a layer of glue and sprinkle with white glitter or salt. Label the surrounding bodies of water and coastal cities.

FARM ON GREENLAND
SEE ERIK THE RED

GREENLAND!?

How did an island covered with ice get a name like Greenland? Erik the Red, a Viking named for his red hair, settled on the island. When Erik the Red was alive, finding a good place to farm was ideal. He wanted to tempt other Viking farmers to settle there too, so he named the island Greenland. Discuss what would be ideal about a place to live today, and write new names and slogans on sentence strips. Post the new names for Greenland and vote for the most effective name.

DID YOU KNOW?

❀ The Hawaiian Islands were formed by erupting volcanoes. Over time, pressure and heat caused liquid rock to form under the Earth's crust. When the volcanoes erupted, they released hot, liquid rock (*magma*) which built up as it was cooled by the ocean.

❀ The magma formed mountainous islands which eventually rose above sea level.

❀ The Hawaiian Islands are a chain of islands called an *archipelago*.

❀ Hawaii, the last state admitted to the United States, is located in the middle of the Pacific Ocean. Its tropical weather and beautiful scenery make it an ideal vacation spot.

CHAIN OF BEAUTY

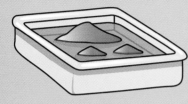

Have a blast making a volcanic island chain just like the archipelago in Hawaii! Fill a shallow tub half-full with water. Using waterproof modeling clay, make a volcanic shape that barely breaks the surface of the water. Add more clay to the top, watching the island grow higher and higher above sea level, and repeat the process for other islands. When there are at least three islands, name the new island chain.

A REAL HOT SPOT

Simulate the force of volcanic reactions with this chemical experiment. Have small groups each model a clay volcano, complete with a 3"-deep hole in the top (don't plan to reuse the clay after this experiment). Give each group a few spoonfuls of baking soda and a cup of vinegar mixed with several drops of red food coloring. Put one teaspoon of baking soda in the top of the "volcano," then add one teaspoon of the vinegar/food coloring mixture to the baking soda. Record observations about the exciting reaction and the steps leading up to it! After the volcano "erupts," repeat this process several times using different amounts of vinegar and baking soda. See who can cause the biggest lava spill.

DANCE ME A STORY

How do you tell a story without saying a word? With the hula! The hula is a traditional Hawaiian dance which uses body and hand movements to tell stories about history, love, and nature. Hula dancers often wear knee-length skirts made from leaves and grasses—in the past, Hawaiians used what was available on the island! Make grass skirts by stapling long strips of newspaper close together across a band of paper large enough to fit around a student's waist. When the bands are finished, turn them inside-out so ends of the strips do not show and staple them around students' hips. Let students work in groups to write and perform story dances. As a class, guess what each story was about, then let students tell their stories to see how accurate the guesses were.

BEAUTIFUL BLOSSOMS

Many of Hawaii's native flowers are not found anywhere else in the world. Hawaiians weave flowers, along with shells, feathers, and whales' teeth, into lovely necklaces called *leis*. Leis are given as symbols of friendship, welcome, and affection. Each island in Hawaii has its own official lei. Make leis by stringing feathers, pasta, and tissue-paper or craft flowers into a pattern. Let students put finished leis around each others' necks and say *"Aloha,"* a Hawaiian greeting!

THE OUTER BANKS, NC
SEDIMENTARY ISLANDS

DID YOU KNOW ?

- The Outer Banks are sedimentary islands. They were formed as wind and water deposited sand (sediment) off the coast. The sand gradually built up to form islands.
- The Outer Banks are a group of narrow islands lining the North Carolina coast. They are called barrier islands because they create a protective barrier between the coast and the ocean.
- The Outer Banks have a rich history; they were the home of Virginia Dare, the first English child born in America, as well as the site of the Wright brothers' first flight.

AN ISLAND OF MY OWN

Demonstrate how to make sedimentary islands with this fast-forward process. Provide the bottom half of a clear, 20-ounce bottle with blue paper for each child. Cover it with blue paper cut in scallops along the top to look like waves. Pour different colors of sand, one layer at a time, into the bottle, until the island begins to rise above "sea level." Add palm tree patterns (page 47) and shells to the sand to complete the island.

THIS LITTLE LIGHT OF MINE

Shallow water around the Outer Banks has caused so many ships to wreck over the years that the area is called *The Graveyard of the Atlantic*. Eventually, several lighthouses were erected to help sailors navigate the dangerous waters. Each lighthouse was uniquely designed and painted to represent its island. The Cape Hatteras lighthouse, which was moved to protect it from a receding coastline, is the tallest lighthouse in the United States. Paint cardboard tubes to look like lighthouses, then cut out two rectangular panels from the tops of the tubes. Tape yellow plastic wrap on the inside, covering the panels, to look like light. Cut out several long, narrow island shapes from brown paper, place them on a table covered with blue paper, and place the cardboard lighthouses among the islands. For added fun, place a small flashlight into some of the lighthouses to really see them shine.

SHIVER ME TIMBERS!

Have some swashbuckling dramatic fun with pirates. Describe some of the more famous pirates, including Blackbeard and Anne Bonny, who hid out in the shallow waters along the Outer Banks. These pirates often raided ships that wrecked around the islands. Let students work in small groups to write pirate adventure skits, create pirate costumes (paper grocery bags with cut-out neck- and armholes work well for this), and perform for parents and other students.

THE FLORIDA KEYS:
CORAL ISLANDS

DID YOU KNOW ?

The Florida Keys formed because thousands of tiny animals called coral polyps built their homes on top of each other. The groups of polyps eventually formed *reefs*, which later grew into islands.

The Keys, located off the southern coast of Florida, stretch for 150 miles and include more than 400 islands. Thirty of these islands are connected by the Overseas Highway (Highway 1).

Many scuba divers and vacationers visit the Keys to enjoy the sea life around the reefs.

CORAL MURAL

Create an undersea garden to see how coral grows into islands. Coral polyps grow into beautiful shapes and patterns called reefs. List the names of different types of coral, such as elkhorn coral, sea fans, and fire coral, and imagine what these different types of coral may look like. Place a large sheet of butcher paper on an art table. Give each student a small piece of sponge to be his coral polyp and have him sponge paint one of the types of coral as he thinks it would look. Display the paintings together on a bulletin board to form a giant coral reef. If possible, show pictures of real coral after the drawings are complete.

FANTASY FISH

Have you ever seen a fish with a crown? How about a shrimp that cuts hair? Coral reefs become the homes for many unusual creatures, which are often named for their colorful markings and interesting shapes. Look at pictures of reef dwellers such as parrot fish, clown fish, queen angelfish, spiny lobsters, flamingo tongues, and barberpole shrimp. Then, let students paint exaggerated versions of these animals based on their names. For example, a clown fish might have big shoes and a red nose. Cut out the creatures and display them on the bulletin board from the *Coral Mural* (above).

GROWING AN ISLAND PARADISE

Many people consider the Florida Keys a paradise—and a very precious one, since they took so long to form! Duplicate the gradual growing process of this coral paradise. Tape blue butcher paper onto a table. Glue a few foam packing chips to the paper every day, until the packing pieces rise above a predetermined "sea level." Stress that just like real coral, this coral is fragile and easily broken. As the area above sea level grows larger, top the surface with palm tree patterns (page 47), and paper animals and people. To expand the activity, draw a map of the new islands, indicating where towns and cities will form. Attach index cards describing the local flora and fauna, then add a longitude and latitude so you can "locate" the island on a larger map!

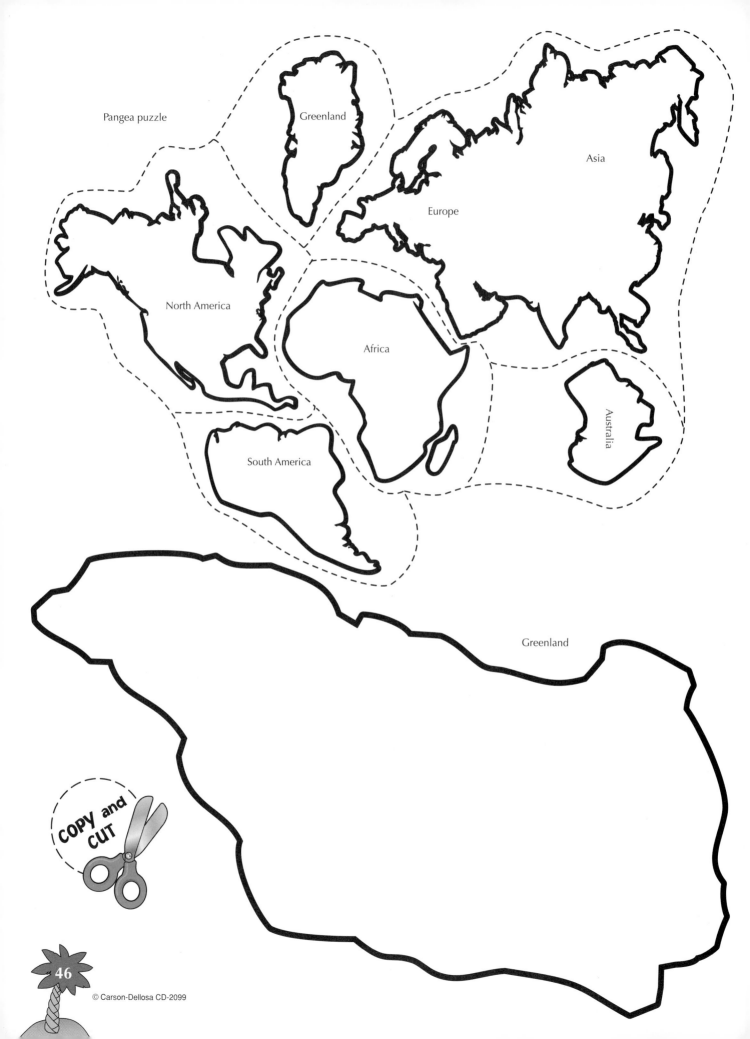

Pangea puzzle

Greenland

Asia

Europe

North America

Africa

Australia

South America

Greenland

COPY and CUT

46

palm tree
(also use with bulletin board idea, page 23)

treasure chest
(use with bulletin board idea, page 23)

47

SHIPS AHOY!

Boats and ships take countless people on new adventures. Share the sense of boating adventure with your class as you take them on the water.

Did You Know?

- Until recently, ornate figureheads were carved into the bows (fronts) of large ships as good luck charms or to show the names of the ships.

- The internationally recognized distress symbol, SOS, stands for *save our souls.*

Literature Selections

Ferryboat Ride! by Anne F. Rockwell: Crown Pub., 1999. (Picture book, 40 pg.) A fun account of a little girl's first ferry ride.

Harbor by Donald Crews: William Morrow and Co., 1987. (Picture book, 32 pg.) Introduces young readers to different types of boats that sail in and out of a harbor.

My Blue Boat by Chris L. Demarest: Voyager Picture Book, 1998. (Picture book, 32 pg.) A girl takes her bath boat on a make-believe ocean adventure.

All Aboard!

Sail into your unit about boats by making a class-sized version of a voyager ship. Place a refrigerator box on its side, cut off the top, cut a long strip from the top piece to form a mast, and tape the mast to one side of the boat using packing tape. Cut a large triangle from butcher paper and tape it to the mast to represent a sail. Cut holes along the sides to represent portholes. Then, provide pictures of boats or use the *Parts of a Boat* diagram (page 52) for small groups of students to use as reference as they add details to the boat. When the boat is complete, vote on a name, paint or draw the name on the side, and "christen" the boat with a plastic bottle. Inside the boat, set up a reading center with books about boats or provide materials from *Learn the Ropes* (page 50).

KNOT CENTER

What Floats Your Boat?

How do boats made of heavy iron and steel stay afloat in the water? Answer the question with this critical thinking activity. Drop a 2" ball of clay into a small, plastic tub about ¾ full of water. Does it float? Let children figure out how to make the clay into a boat that will float. (Flatten it into a bowl shape; the more water surface area the clay covers, the better it will float). Explain that water pushes against objects, supporting them so they can float. When the clay was in a ball, there was not enough water under the ball to hold it up. When the clay is spread out over the surface of the water, more water pushes up the clay, allowing it to float.

Ship to Shore

Communicating with dots and dashes is easy once you know the code! Sailors can communicate with other ships and people on land with a code system transmitted by radio (the code is represented either by sounds or by dots and dashes). This system, called *Morse code* after its inventor, Samuel B. Morse, was designed so people could communicate telegraphs over long distances before the telephone was invented. Look up Morse code in the encyclopedia to get a copy of the code. Dashes represent long sounds, while dots represent shorter sounds. Tap out the code for SOS, or say *dot dot dot, dash dash dash, dot dot dot* (Morse code for SOS). Challenge students to tap out their names. Let students write their names in Morse code on construction paper and glue a string (rope) border around the paper. You may wish to write a message in Morse code on the chalkboard each morning during this unit.

Julie

Todd

Pam

Ship Shape

After making this silhouette book, students will be able to identify ships by their shapes! Let each child color and cut out the six boat patterns (page 53), then trace them onto black construction paper and cut them out again. Glue each black shape to a half sheet of blue construction paper, then glue the colorful boats on the backs of the construction paper sheets, matching each boat to its corresponding shape. At the bottom of each silhouette page, write *What shape is this?* Label the boat on each colorful page. If desired, write sentences about how each boat is powered, where it travels, or how it is used. Create a cover for the book, arrange the pages so that each silhouette is facing up, then staple the book together along the left side. For an extra nautical effect, punch holes in the sheets and tie the book together with string in sailor's knots.

An Ocean Liner!

What shape is this?

Safety First

Keep students from going overboard with this lifesaving booklet. Go over the safety guidelines for water fun (listed at right) with the class. Have each student draw a 4" circle in the middle of seven 8" white circles. Cut out the center circles. Color opposite sections of each circle red to look like a life preserver. Students can write one water safety rule on each preserver in the white spaces and use the eighth preserver as a cover. Stack the preservers and punch a hole at the top. Then, punch seven more holes in the cover, spacing them equally apart. Start at a hole beside the top hole and thread a red, curling ribbon through the holes, always lacing down. At the top hole, thread the rings together. Tie the ribbon ends together. Hang the life preservers in the classroom.

Amy's

Water Safety Book

SAFETY RULES

- Never swim or go boating in bad weather.
- Always wear a life preserver when boating.
- Always swim with a buddy under adult supervision.
- Never dive into unfamiliar water.
- Swim only in approved areas.
- If someone is in trouble in the water, throw them a flotation device and get help.
- Do not swim near moving boats.

Learn the Ropes

Teach your students to tie up loose ends! Sailors must learn to tie different knots for a variety of purposes. Some knots are meant to be permanent, while others are meant to slip and untie easily. Copy diagrams and instructions for tying some simple knots. Use an encyclopedia, a book on knot tying, or check out knot-tying sites on the Internet for reference. Knots such as the *overhand, figure eight, square (with two ropes), half hitch (tie around a chair leg or pole), simple slip knot,* and *clove hitch* are easiest for little hands to tie. Place the diagrams and instructions at a center, along with several lengths of rope (jump ropes without handles work well) and let students try this essential sailing skill. You may wish to supply a ball of string so students may tie their favorite knots to take home with them.

Bottle It!

Constructing miniature models of boats inside bottles was a popular craft with sailors in the mid-19th century. Models were painstakingly built by constructing as much of the boat as possible outside of the bottle, then erecting the sails and finishing the details using tiny tools pushed in the bottle opening. Make a ship in a bottle the easy way by using a craft knife to cut a 4" vertical slit into the side of a plastic 20-ounce soda bottle. Have each child draw, color, and cut out a ship on a 3" x 4" piece of white paper, leaving a 1/2" tab of paper at the bottom. Color the other side of the ship after it has been cut out. Bend the tab along the bottom, then slide the ship through the slit in the bottle so the tab is still on the outside of the slit. Use clear tape to attach the tab to the outside of the bottle, then place a pencil in the bottle and bend the ship to make it stand up straight. Replace the bottle caps and let each student amaze her friends with her ship in a bottle!

Aye Aye, Captain!

Teach little sailors the meanings of the boating words listed. Let them practice using the words until they are familiar with them (raising their *port* hand, etc.). Then, play *Captain Says*, played like *Simon Says*, using boating directions. Be the captain and give directions such as *Lift your starboard foot to the stern* (each student would lift his right foot behind him). Play several rounds, allowing the last player eliminated to be the next captain.

Stern

Starboard

Port

Come About

Capsize

Bow

Vitamin C Boats

"C" your way to good health with this delicious seaworthy snack. Fresh fruits and vegetables did not last on long voyages with no refrigeration, so many sailors developed *scurvy*, a Vitamin C deficiency. Keep your sailors from getting scurvy during their boating adventures with these vitamin C-packed boats. Thread a pretzel stick through a triangular piece of fruit leather, creating a sail, then push the other end of the pretzel into an orange slice. Enjoy the boats after the *Whatta Regatta*, below.

Life Jacket Relay

Stay afloat with this fun life preserver game! Provide two life jackets in a child's size (check with the local YMCA, community pool, or other child aquatics program to borrow life jackets). Use a volunteer to demonstrate how to put on the life jacket. Divide the class into two teams, and give each team a life jacket. Line up the team members and take turns putting on the life jacket, taking it off, and passing it to the next player. The first team to finish correctly putting on the life jacket is the winning team!

S.S. Karl

Celebrate your *Ships Ahoy!* studies with a parade of beautiful boats. Gather large cardboard boxes and use them to design children's boat costumes to wear during the parade. Create suspenders from shoelaces or string to hold up the boats. Cut out portholes, make crow's nest hats, even use cardboard tubes to make submarine periscopes! Invite other classes to watch the cardboard boat regatta. If desired, group the boats by type, such as canoes, yachts, etc. After the regatta, you may wish to play *Captain Says* (see *Aye Aye, Captain*, above) with your class, and enjoy the *Vitamin C Boats* (above).

Parts of a Boat

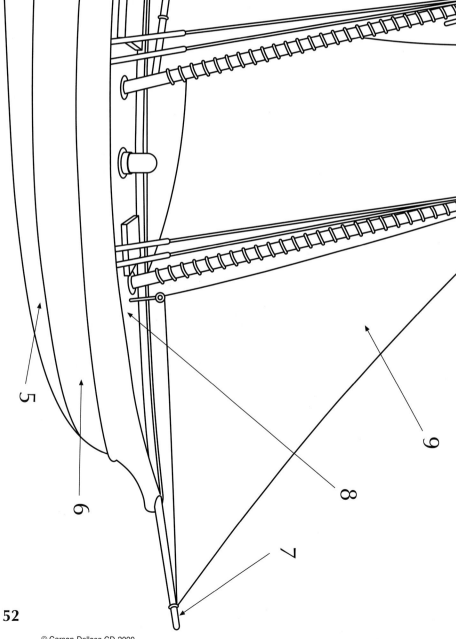

1 boom	6 hull		
2 stern	7 bow		
3 tiller	8 deck		
4 rudder	9 sail		
5 keel	10 mast		

canoe

ocean liner

ferry

COPY and CUT

sailboat

speedboat

submarine

53

CAMP LOTS-O-FUN

Pack your backpacks, fill your canteens, and get ready to go on a camping adventure! Filling your classroom with the inviting atmosphere of the great outdoors is sure to have your students hitting the trail and clamoring with "in-tents" excitement!

Literature Selections

Arthur Goes to Camp by Marc Brown: Little Brown and Co., 1984. (Picture book, 32 pg.) Arthur decides he wants to run away from summer camp.

Crinkleroot's Guide to Walking in Wild Places by Jim Arnosky: Aladdin Paperbacks, 1993. (Picture book, 32 pg.) Crinkleroot lives in the forest and gives tips for forest and wilderness safety.

The Kids Campfire Book by Jane Drake: Kids Can Press, 1998. (Reference book, 128 pg.) Helpful resource that includes campfire songs, games, and recipes.

Did You Know?

🔥 Campsites were commonly used by cowboys and explorers as a place to bed down while traveling.

🔥 Native Americans were the first true campers in North America. They learned to hunt, fish, and live comfortably in the wilderness.

Campsite Snapshots

Students can design picture perfect campsites with this art project. Provide catalogs that offer camping and other outdoor supplies and equipment. Pass out pieces of 8" x 8" oaktag or poster board, and let students glue cut-out pictures of camping equipment to the paper to create a campsite scene. Add details with markers or crayons. To make the pictures resemble snapshots, leave a plain border around the pictures and color the corners brown or black to look as if they have been placed in a photo album. Display the snapshots on a bulletin board. If desired, write camping captions beneath them.

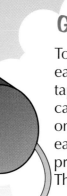

Guess What We Saw When We Went Hiking?

To find out, play a guessing game using handmade binoculars. Have each child attach two short cardboard tubes together with masking tape to resemble binoculars. Sponge-paint the binoculars in camouflage greens and browns. To create a neck strap, punch a hole on the outside of each tube and thread one end of a long string into each hole. Tie a knot to secure the string. To use the binoculars, pretend to "hike" through the classroom and play a game of *I Spy*. The catch is, players must always "spy" through their binoculars!

Happy Trails Mix

This tasty treat is sure to bring lots of smiles as your campers hike those miles. Use a clean, plastic container with a handle to hold your mix (quart-sized milk jugs and small syrup bottles work well). Use a measuring cup to measure $1/4$ cup raisins, $1/4$ cup peanuts, and $1/2$ cup granola. Pour each ingredient through a funnel into the bottle. Shake the bottle to mix the ingredients, replace the lid, then loop a string through the handle to create a waist belt.

Letters From Camp

Give book reports a new twist—have children write them as letters from camp. Begin by setting up a small tent in your classroom (a makeshift tent can be made by folding a sheet over a table). Place camping items such as a flashlight, a canteen, and a couple of sleeping bags in the tent, along with assorted books about camping. Let children take turns reading the books in the tent, then writing short book reports as letters, describing the characters, setting, and plot to someone. Students can share their letters from camp with other classroom campers.

Dear Mom, Here is my Book Report.

What Are You Reading in **Your** Tent?

Expand on the sure-to-be-popular idea of reading tents as you create ideal, quiet, reading spaces for a whole week! Ask parents to donate a few tents to the classroom, or use the sheet-and-table suggestion from *Letters from Camp,* above. Assign one genre, such as mystery, adventure, biography, etc., to each tent. Hang a corresponding sign for each genre on a different tent. Stock the tents with appropriate books, and have children visit them during free time. Groups can visit if there is enough room. Make sure to provide flashlights to light up those cozy spaces!

Tall Campfire Tales

One of the best parts of camping is...scary campfire stories!
On the classroom floor, arrange rocks, small logs, and
twigs to resemble a campfire. Cut orange and yellow flames
from tissue paper. Gather around the fire and turn off
the lights. Place marshmallows on craft sticks and
"roast" them over the campfire. Start a story by saying,
"It was a dark and stormy night. We had just gotten
into our tent when...." Then, choose a child to add
a sentence or two to the story. Continue around
the circle adding sentences to the story. For added
fun, tape the story and replay it to remind
children of their camping adventures.

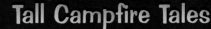

Scrumptious S'mores

Your students will be asking for
more—just like the name implies!
Spread marshmallow cream on a
graham cracker, add a section of
chocolate bar or chocolate chips,
then top with another cracker.
Gather around the classroom
campfire and sing camp songs as
you enjoy these treats!

Make Tracks on the Wild Side

This activity will leave a lasting impression on your class!
By identifying animal tracks, campers can find out what
kinds of animals are in the area. Provide a reference book
which shows different tracks. Give each child some
modeling clay and have her make up a new animal, then
design its track in the clay. Have the children write sentences
describing the animals, draw illustrations of them, and
name the new creatures they tracked and found!

tiger monkey

Careful Campers

A prepared and cautious camper is a happy camper. Brainstorm a list of possible camping problems, such as mosquitoes, sunburn, etc. Copy the *Campers' First Aid Guide* (page 59) for each student. Let each child cut out the sections and staple them together in order. Assign groups and give each group a first aid topic to research. Provide reference on poisonous or troublesome plants, sunburns, bites and stings, cuts and scrapes, minor sprains, etc. As each group finishes its research, have students add information to the blank backs of the pages in their books, creating a first aid and prevention guide for each topic. When all of the guides are complete, read them as a class, then finish the activity by brainstorming another list—this time, of what should be in every camper's first aid kit!

All Signs Point to...Safety!

Your class will "sign up" for safety with these reminders. Copy the *Camping Safety Rules* (page 58). Cut them apart, and assign them to small groups. Let groups write slogans for their rules on large pieces of oaktag, then use art supplies, twigs, leaves, and other outdoor objects to illustrate the posters. Display the posters around your campfire from *Tall Campfire Tales* (page 56).

Traveling Tents

As classroom camp draws to a close, pass the fun along to other potential campers by creating travel brochures designed to sing the praises of camping. Fold a sheet of construction paper in half to resemble a tent, then have children write and illustrate all the great things they experienced in their classroom camp! Post the tents on a bulletin board and lift the tent flaps to read about great camping experiences.

57

Do not eat plants or berries you find while camping or hiking.

Watch where you step and climb.

Never leave a campfire unattended.

Use water and dirt to completely extinguish a campfire.

Do not drink water from lakes, rivers, or streams.

Never hike alone.

Always carry a first aid kit on camping trips.

Pack weather-appropriate clothing for your trip.

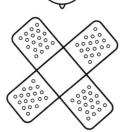

Campers' First Aid Guide

How to prevent getting a rash from poisonous plants:

Wear long-sleeved clothing and long pants when hiking. Wash hands often. Learn how to recognize poisonous plants and avoid them.

What to do if you get a rash:

Wash the affected area and put anti-itch lotion on it. DO NOT SCRATCH!

1

How to prevent sunburn:

Avoid the sun between 10:00 and 2:00. Wear sunscreen and a hat during outdoor activities.

What to do if you get a sunburn:

Drink plenty of water. Put lotion with aloe on your skin. If blisters develop, see a doctor.

2

How to prevent insect bites:

Wear long-sleeved clothing and long pants when hiking. Do not wear scented deodorant or perfume. Use insect repellant. Avoid swampy or damp areas.

What to do if you get insect bites:

DO NOT SCRATCH! Apply an anti-itch lotion.

3

How to prevent bee stings:

Do not swat at bees. Avoid colorful clothing.

What to do if you get a bee sting:

If mild swelling occurs, take an over-the-counter antihistamine pill. Avoid scratching the sting.

4

How to prevent scrapes and cuts:

Wear a long-sleeved shirt and long pants when hiking. Make sure you have the right footgear for the kind of trail you are hiking on.

What to do if you get a cut:

Wash the area well. Put antibacterial cream on the cut and cover with a bandage.

5

High Flying Flag Fun!

On Flag Day (June 14), unfurl students' enthusiasm for flags: state, national, international, even signal flags, and learn about their designs and histories!

Did You Know?

▷ A *vexillologist* studies the history of flags and their designs. Flags symbolize many things, such as pride, loyalty, and hope.

▷ The *canton* is the blue part of the American flag. The *field* is the striped part of the flag. The side of the flag that is attached to the flag pole is the *hoist*.

▷ Popular legend has it that Betsy Ross, a seamstress who designed flags for the Navy, helped General George Washington design the American flag, but no one knows for sure who really designed the American flag.

▷ Many organizations, such as the Red Cross and the Olympic Games, have flags designed specifically for them with their own symbols and colors.

▷ Ships at sea often use international signal flags to communicate with each other.

Literature Selections

A Flag for Our Country by Eve Spencer: Raintree/Steck-Vaughn, 1996. (Storybook, 32 pg.) Informative book about Betsy Ross and Flag Day.
I Know About Flags by Chris Jaeggi: Rand McNally & Co., 1995. (Picture book, 24 pg.) Easy-to-read book with pictures and information about many types of flags.
The Star-Spangled Banner by Peter Spier: Yearling Books, 1992. (Picture book, 56 pg.) Illustrated rendering of the first, second, and third versions of Francis Scott Key's song.

In Search of Flags

Flags are everywhere, especially when you go on a flag hunt! Treat students to some indoor-outdoor fun searching for flags. Draw, cut out, or copy a variety of flags, such as country flags, state or province flags, organization flags, even a pirate flag or a racing (checkered) flag. Write each flag's name and description on a corresponding index card. Hide the flags around the classroom or playground (place flags hidden outside in resealable plastic bags with a few rocks, to prevent them from blowing away). Pass out the index cards, and let the flag-capturing commence!

60

A Stitch In Time

The United States Congress officially adopted the stars and stripes of the United States flag on June 14, 1777, but no one knows for sure how the design was created. Encourage students to make up their own legends about how the flag was created. Let groups work cooperatively to write plays about the legend of the making of the first American flag, then perform the plays for the class.

Seamstress for a Day!

Students can pretend they are sewing their own American flags without even lifting a needle! Each design on the flag has its own meaning. The 50 stars represent the 50 states, and the 13 red and white stripes represent the original 13 colonies. The colors have meaning as well: red represents hardiness and valor, white stands for purity and innocence, and blue represents vigilance, perseverance, and justice. To make realistic handmade flags, glue seven strips of red felt to a white, rectangular felt background, starting and ending with a red stripe. Then, glue a blue rectangle over the red strips in the top left corner. Complete the flag by adding a circle of 13 small, white star stickers to the blue rectangle. Finished flags can be attached to drinking straws or dowel rods for students to proudly display.

A Flag by Any Other Name...

Old Glory, Star-Spangled Banner, Stars and Stripes...these are some of the nicknames for the American flag. The name *Old Glory* is said to have been coined by a sea captain named William Driver. Before he left on a sea voyage, friends gave him an American flag as a gift. He raised the flag on his ship and called it *Old Glory*. Look at an American flag and think about what the colors and design represent (see *Seamstress for a Day*, above). What other nicknames could the American flag be given? Let students think of new nicknames for the flag and write them on small rectangles, along with stories about the nicknames. Post the stories around the classroom, in a reading center, or right beneath your classroom flag!

Old Glory

All Shapes and Sizes

Like the United States, other countries have different flags that are unique to their histories. Have each student research another country's flag, then use the colors and symbols to create a new flag. Make a large outline of each researched country on a rectangular sheet of paper. Using a pictorial reference of each country's flag, copy the basic symbols and shapes of the flag inside of the outline. Add a few facts about the country around the edges of the outline. Write the name of each country on the back of its new "flag." Post the flags and see who can guess the corresponding countries.

THE GREAT BARRIER REEF IS LOCATED OFF THE COAST.

THE PLATYPUS LIVES HERE.

KANGAROOS, KOALAS, WOMBATS, AND WALLABIES LIVE HERE.

THE OUTBACK IS IN THIS COUNTRY.

The Tarheel State

Special Flags for Special States

Countries are not the only places that have flags— states have flags too! Design a new flag for your state. Let students research the state bird, state song, state flower, state tree, state nickname, and state motto, and incorporate some or all of these symbols into a state flag. Display a real state flag for students to compare to their flags.

Spell Your Name With Flags!

Flag fun will abound when children use signal flags for spelling! Explain that 26 flags, each corresponding to a letter of the English alphabet, are part of an international code used by ships to communicate at sea. Display the signal flags (page 63). Have students look at the code and locate the flags which represent the letters in their names, then draw and color their flag names on sheets of paper. For a memory challenge, hold up the flag name papers one at a time and see who can guess each name shown.

M   I   K   E   Y

Let's Make a Five-Pointed Star!

Many states and countries use 5-, 6-, even 7-pointed stars in their flags! Flag makers and seamstresses have a special, simple, and timesaving way to cut out 5-pointed stars. Give each student a copy of the five-pointed star diagram (page 63) and an 8" x 8" piece of paper, along with the directions for creating 5-pointed stars. Students can work together to create a class flag which incorporates 5-pointed stars.

Step 1
Fold a sheet of paper in half as shown.

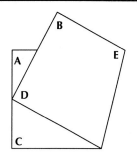

Step 2
Fold the paper again so that Point D is between Point A and Point C.

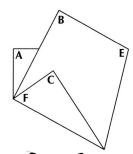

Step 3
Fold up Point C to create Point F.

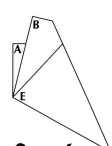

Step 4
Fold Point E down to Point F.

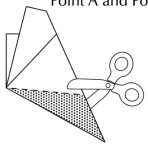

Step 5
Cut a line from Point E to the opposite edge.

Step 6
Unfold your star!

International Code Flags

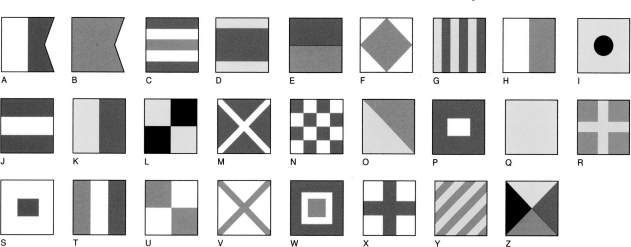

Father's Day
A Tribute to Dads

Preparing for Father's Day can provide many learning opportunities in the classroom. As students are encouraged to honor their fathers, they also will learn to express their feelings in writing and enjoy art and craft activities. Children can honor fathers, stepfathers, uncles, or grandfathers.

Did You Know?

◇ Sonora Dodd of Washington first proposed the idea of a *Father's Day* in 1909, to honor the strength, courage, and selflessness of her father, William Smart. Sonora's father, a Civil War veteran, raised his six children alone after his wife died in childbirth.

◇ The first Father's Day in the United States was observed on June 19, 1910 in Spokane, Washington.

◇ In 1966, President Lyndon Johnson signed a presidential proclamation declaring the third Sunday of June as Father's Day.

Literature Selections

◇ *All Dads on Deck* by Judy Delton: Young Yearling, 1994. (Storybook, 88 pg.) A group of scouts plans a fishing excursion in honor of Father's Day. One of them comes up with a plan to ensure that no fish are hurt.

◇ *Just Like My Dad* by Tricia Gardella: HarperCollins: 1996. (Picture book, 32 pg.) This story of life on a ranch with a cowboy dad is told from the child's point of view. A gentle celebration of the special relationship between father and child.

◇ *Pinky and Rex and the Double-Dad Weekend* by James Howe: Atheneum, 1995. (Picture book, 48 pg.) Pinky and Rex's long awaited camping trip with their dads is rained out, but they manage to have a fun-filled weekend "camping in."

♪ ♫ Singing for Dad ♫ ♪

Teach children to sing the following song to the tune of *If You're Happy and You Know It*. Remind children to sing this song to their dads on Father's Day or any day!

I'm So Happy You're My Dad

I'm so happy you're my dad, I love you!
I'm so happy you're my dad, I love you!
You're the best that there could be,
I can tell that you love me,
I'm so happy you're my dad, I love you!

Dear Amazing Dad

Children can focus on special attributes of their dads by writing acrostic poems using their dads' first names (or first and last names). Instruct each student to write a name poem similar to the one at right, using each letter in her dad's name to state why he is special. Encourage children to make the poems personal by thinking about their dads' hobbies or things that their dads do with them. Have students illustrate their poems and use them in Father's Day cards, or include them with their *Gift Cards* (see below).

James is my dad
Always makes me laugh
Makes yummy sandwiches
Every Saturday
So glad he's my dad!

Happy Father's Day!

Gift Cards

Let each student make a card for dad that includes a little something extra! Encourage children to think about something special they could do for their dads on Father's Day, such as making his favorite sandwich or cleaning out his car. Provide a 5" x 7" piece of poster board for each child. Instruct students to write Father's Day messages on the cards, noting their special gifts. Students can also draw items that remind them of their fathers, such as footballs, books, or hearts!

Picture This!

I Love you Dad!
– Anna

A wallet-sized photograph, poster board, and a few craft materials can make a charming picture frame that will delight any dad! Let each child trace a 5" x 7" shape onto poster board (for the backing), and trace the same shape on either wrapping or construction paper (for the matting). Cut out a heart shape in the matting material to hold a photograph of the child. Have students write the date or a personal message to dad. Buttons or shapes cut from paper or felt could be glued on also. Let children glue or tape a wallet-sized picture of themselves in place, and then glue the matting onto the poster board. Ribbon can be glued around the edge of the poster board for a finishing touch! Dads can prop the picture on a desk or table, use sticky-tack to attach it to a wall, or frame it.

65

Bird's Nest Cookies for Dad

Let each child say "I love you, dad!" by presenting her father with a bird's nest cookie and a personal note inside an attractive bag! Children can use markers, crayons, glitter, and sequins to decorate the paper lunch bags.

Ingredients:
4 cups chow mein noodles
4 cups flaked cereal, coarsely crushed
32 ounces white chocolate or vanilla flavored candy coating
2/3 cup small jelly beans

Have children help you using the following directions:

- Spread waxed paper over your work surface. Combine the noodles and cereal in a large bowl and set aside.

- Melt the white chocolate or candy-coating in a double boiler over hot water or in a microwave oven. Stir until smooth. Remove from heat and pour over the noodle and cereal mixture.

- To form bird's nests, mound two tablespoons of the mixture onto the waxed paper. With the back of a teaspoon, make an indentation in the center of each mound. Press a few jelly beans in the center of each nest. Allow to set at room temperature until firm. When the cookies have cooled, allow each child to wrap a cookie in waxed paper or colored cellophane and place in a decorated bag along with a personal note to dad!

Shaped Books

What dad wouldn't like a shaped book for Father's Day from his favorite author? From poster board, children can cut out shapes that remind them of their dads, such as a briefcase, tool box, football, etc. Use these shapes as templates from which to cut the inside pages. In the books, have children write or illustrate why their dads are great!

Dad Mobile

Let each student create a mobile that represents a few of his dad's favorite things. Write the letters D-A-D on an 8¹/₂" x 11" sheet of poster board in large, overlapping letters. Color or decorate the letters and then cut off the surrounding paper. On a separate sheet of poster board, have children draw, color, and cut out pictures of objects that remind them of their dads, such as sports equipment, gardening tools, books, etc. Punch holes in the poster board pieces and use yarn to hang the pictures from the letters, along with other small, real objects such as washers, screws, photos, dried flowers, etc. Make the mobile ready for Dad to display by punching a hole in the top of each letter and attaching a yarn hanger as shown.

Papier-Mâché Bowl

Dads can use this bowl for holding keys, loose change, or other items. Provide each child with a small plastic foam bowl to use as a mold. Cover the outsides and rims of the bowls with plastic wrap. Smooth the wrap, pull it tight, and tape it to the insides of the bowls. Protect tables with newspapers and let children work on sheets of waxed paper. Have children tear newspapers into small squares or rectangles. Demonstrate how to dip a piece of newspaper into papier-mâché paste and remove excess paste by running the paper between your fingers. Instruct children to start at the rim, laying a piece of paper onto the bowl and smoothing it. Repeat this process around the rim, being careful to slightly overlap the pieces. When the rim is finished, cover the rest of the bowl with paper. Repeat six times, allowing the paper to dry each time (this could take 10-20 minutes for each layer). Allow to dry for at least 12 hours. Remove the bowls from the forms and let students paint them when completely dry.

Papier-Mâché Paste

Mix 2-3 cups of water for every 1 cup of flour. Stir well to create a slightly thick, smooth paste.

67

Graduation: A Stepping Stone

Graduation not only signifies an end, it represents a commencement—a new beginning! Use the activities in this chapter to recognize and celebrate students' personal achievements and the successful completion of the school year.

Did You Know?

- Graduates in the United States, Canada, and Great Britain wear hats called mortarboards. In France, a graduate's hat looks something like a chef's hat. In Spain, a woman graduate wears headgear resembling a Tiffany lamp shade—a blue satin bowl covered with tiny glass beads!
- Traditionally, candidates for graduation wear their tassels on the front right side of their caps and move them to the left when awarded a diploma.
- Graduates often march to the stately song *Pomp and Circumstance* by Sir Edward Elgar (1857-1934).

Regalia!

Distinguished graduates should dress the part! Provide students with graduation certificates and let them make mortarboard caps and graduation sashes to wear on their special day!

- ***Certificates and Awards*** Provide each student with a graduation certificate and honor special students with awards for achievement using the patterns on pages 16-17.
- ***Mortarboards*** Cut a 2"-wide strip of poster board long enough to go around each child's head. Cut a 9" square from poster board for the top of his cap. If desired, let each student decorate his cap. Use hot glue to attach the cap to the head band. Insert a paper fastener into the center top of the cap. For the tassel, cut three 24" pieces of yarn for each cap. Hold the yarn-ends together, fold in half, and tie a knot 1" from the folded end. Attach the tassel to the top of the cap by slipping the looped ends under the top of the paper fastener.
- ***Sashes*** Cut a 6"-wide strip of bulletin board paper long enough to make a sash for each child. Each student can decorate and write *Class of 20__* on the front of his sash. Cut the ends into a "V" shape and tape them together.

Graduation Gift

Give each graduating student a scrolled poem or letter as a graduation keepsake! Choose a poem that expresses your feelings for the class or write a letter of congratulations and best wishes. Copy the message onto colorful paper, roll up, and tie each with a ribbon. Distribute this special gift at a graduation party or ceremony. (See page 25 to create a graduation bulletin board using these scrolls.)

Graduation Party

Invite parents to a party honoring the graduates! Serve cookies, cheese and crackers, or other simple snacks along with this quick and easy punch that students can help prepare.

Promotion Punch Ingredients:
2 12-ounce cans frozen concentrated fruit juice, any kind, thawed
3 2-liter bottles ginger ale
1 quart vanilla ice cream or lime sherbet

Directions:
Pour the thawed fruit juice into a punch bowl or large pitcher. Slowly add the ginger ale. Place small scoops of the ice cream or sherbet into the punch. Stir gently. Makes approximately 32 8-ounce servings.

Class Originals

Proclaim the uniqueness of your class by creating class graduation banners! Have each student create a banner containing the name and year of your class and a symbol from a class event or accomplishment. The banners could be made from poster board or fabric and decorated with markers, paint, or felt cut-outs. Stitch or glue a hem along the top to hold a dowel rod and attach yarn for hanging. Display the banners at your graduation party or ceremony.

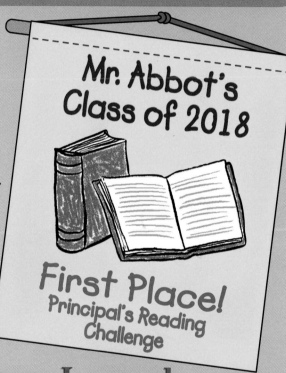

Mr. Abbot's Class of 2018

First Place!
Principal's Reading Challenge

CLASS OF 2015

Tara

Graduation Cap Books

Make a graduation cap autograph book as a special memento of the school year. Provide each student with two 8" squares of poster board and ten 8" squares of white paper. Staple the paper together, using the poster board as front and back covers and then glue a button onto the center of the front cover. Make the tassel as described in *Regalia* (page 68). Attach the tassel to the button with glue or by slipping the looped ends under the button. Instruct each student to write *Class of 20__* and her name on the front cover. Allow children to sign each other's books.

Lessons Learned

Graduates can share their knowledge with the upcoming class by creating a *Words of Wisdom* booklet. Have each student write a paragraph noting things they think would be helpful to your next class—from academic tips to social advice, such as *Listen to the teacher* or *Don't throw things out the bus window*. Display the booklet at your graduation ceremony or party for students and parents to enjoy!

WE ALL SCREAM FOR ICE CREAM!

What's the scoop on ice cream? July is Ice Cream Month. With a sprinkle of history and a helping of fun, these activities will give your class the frosty facts about this tasty treat!

Did You Know?

Ice cream was first made about 2,000 years ago when people mixed honey or fruit with snow.

The first ice cream cone was served at the 1904 World's Fair in St. Louis. When an ice cream vendor ran out of paper dishes, the vendor beside him folded a warm waffle into a cone to create the first "ice cream cornucopia."

Literature Selections

Curious George Goes to an Ice Cream Shop by Margret Rey, H. A. Rey: Houghton Mifflin, 1989. (Picture book, 32 pg.) Curious George samples ice cream in Mr. Herb's store.

Ice Cream Larry by Daniel Pinkwater: Marshall Cavendish Corp., 1999. (Picture book, 32 pg.) Larry the lovable polar bear finds comfort— and a snack—while sleeping in an ice cream store freezer.

Isaac the Ice-Cream Truck by Scott Santoro: Henry Holt & Co., 1999. (Picture book, 32 pg.) An ice cream truck longs to be doing something more important.

It's All in the Name

Give the scoop on ice cream history. How did the name *ice cream sundae* come about? Let your students take a guess. Copy several ice cream scoop patterns (page 73). Draw and cut out bowl shapes, color and glue on the scoops, and add pom-poms, cotton balls, aquarium rocks, glitter, etc., to represent different toppings. On the bowls, write guesses of where the name *sundae* originated. Share the guesses, then reveal the secret: since the first ice cream sundaes were expensive to make, store owners only sold them on Sunday (the most popular day for ice cream) to make sure they would sell enough. Once ice cream sundaes became popular, the spelling of the word *Sunday* was changed to *sundae* so people would know they could enjoy this treat any day of the week.

I think ice cream sundaes are called sundaes because we eat them when it's sunny outside.

70

Flavor of the Day

Originally, ice cream was only available in chocolate, vanilla, and strawberry. Today, ice cream comes in flavors to suit every taste. One company offers 31 flavors of ice cream. Challenge students to come up with 31 different flavors of ice cream by making a list of all the flavors they can think of. Then, instruct small groups to compare lists and cross out any duplicate flavors, replacing them with new ones. Finally, compile a list of all the ice cream flavors. What a tasty assignment!

Fantastically Fun Flavors

Create tasty-looking and tasty-sounding ice cream scoop crafts. Brainstorm flavor names that use alliteration, such as *luscious lemony lime*, or *coconut candy crunch*. Let each child staple two ice cream scoop patterns (page 73) together at the top. On the bottom pattern, write the alliterative flavor name. Color the top pattern to match the name, then glue the scoops to the cone pattern (page 73). Attach finished ice cream cones to a bulletin board and let students try to name the flavors shown, then lift the scoops and read the real names.

How Do the Flavors Stack Up?

Which ice cream flavor is the class favorite? Have a taste test to find out. Bring in containers of chocolate, strawberry, and vanilla ice cream. Post three large cone patterns (page 73) on a bulletin board and label one *chocolate*, one *vanilla*, and one *strawberry*. Let children sample the flavors and choose their favorites. Then, have each child write her name on a scoop pattern (page 73) and color it to correspond with the chosen flavor. Graph the results by posting the scoops on the appropriate cones.

Steps to a Sweet Treat

Everyone should know how to make an ice cream cone! Write helpful how-to guides instructing first-time cone makers how they can make this yummy treat in three easy steps. Accordion-fold a half-sheet of white paper vertically to create four horizontal sections. Draw a cone on the bottom section and draw an ice cream scoop in each remaining section. Write one step to making an ice cream cone on each scoop, starting with the scoop closest to the cone. Color the cone and scoops. Spread a thin layer of glue on the top scoop and add colorful ice cream sprinkles! If desired, color the paper around the ice cream cone and fold the book as shown.

What's on the Menu?

Sundaes, shakes, floats...there are so many delicious ice cream desserts! Explore the choices by letting students make ice cream shop menus on sheets of paper, complete with names of the shop, items, and prices. When the menus are complete, write word problems based on menu items and prices. Staple the word problems to the top of the menu. Let children work in pairs to solve each others' word problems and check the answers.

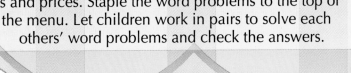

The Magic Scoop
Ice Cream Shop

Banana in a Boat Sundae $3.50
Thick and Frosty Milkshake $2.75
Out of this World Ice Cream Float ... $2.50

Ice Cream Cones
Single Scoop $1.00
Double Scoop $2.00
Triple Scoop $3.00

Toppings:
sprinkles, nuts, hot fudge, pineapples .. 50¢

A Sundae fit for a King $5.50
5 scoops of ice cream topped with sprinkles,
whipped cream, nuts, and hot fudge.

How Many Licks?

How many licks does it take to finish one scoop of ice cream? Treat your class to ice cream and find out! Pass out single-scoop ice cream cones to the class and tally every lick, adding up the total number of licks. Older children can find the average number of licks for the class, while younger children can determine the highest and lowest number of licks in the class.

COOL CONES

These 3-dimensional ice cream cones look good enough to eat! Let each child cut two triangle shapes from a brown paper bag. Decorate one side of each triangle to resemble an ice cream cone. Staple the cones together, leaving the top open. Use paper scraps to stuff the cones, then staple the top shut. Sponge paint the backs of two white paper plates to resemble ice cream, then glue them together to create a scoop. Staple the scoop to the top of the cone, then provide paper, glue, markers, and crayons to add nuts, sprinkles, fruit, etc. Let students pretend to eat the giant ice cream cones!

A Brand New Flavor!

Got an idea for a new ice cream flavor? Let's hear it! Create new flavors and design the packages for the new product. Have students think of new flavors, write flavor descriptions, and list ingredients similar to a list on a real ice cream container. Bring in empty, clean ice cream containers. Have students cover each container with construction paper, then decorate the package. For added fun, write and perform a slogan, jingle, or short commercial describing why everyone simply *must* try each new flavor!

Roly Poly Ice Cream

Enjoy this fun-to-make-and-eat treat in school, or send this recipe home with students. To make six servings, you will need:

1 cup whole milk
1 cup heavy whipping cream
¹/₂ cup sugar
¹/₂ teaspoon vanilla
pinch of salt
rock salt
crushed ice cubes
1 12-ounce coffee can
1 39-ounce coffee can
masking or packing tape

Stir the milk and cream together in a large bowl. Mix in sugar, vanilla, and salt. Pour the mixture in the small coffee can, leaving about 2" between the mixture and the top of the can. Put the lid on the small can, and create a tight seal by taping the lid shut. Place the small can inside the large can, and add 1¹/₂ cups of crushed ice around the small can. Then, add several handfuls of rock salt. Continue adding layers of crushed ice and rock salt to the large can until it is full. Place the lid on the large can. Roll the can back and forth on a sidewalk, floor, or blacktop for about 20-25 minutes. When you open the small can, you should have ice cream!

ice cream scoop
(also use with
bulletin board
idea pg. 25)

COPY and CUT

ice cream cone
(also use with
bulletin board
idea pg. 25)

73

Happy Birthday USA!

Raise your flags, ready your fireworks, and let the parade begin for Independence Day! Take your class through a patriotic journey of fun facts, historic information, and traditional songs as you celebrate freedom and the Fourth!

Did You Know?

- On July 4th, 1776, the United States adopted the *Declaration of Independence*, announcing that the United States was free from British rule.
- On July 8, 1776, the first celebration of independence was held in Philadelphia, where the town rang the Liberty Bell to summon people to hear a public reading of the *Declaration of Independence*. The bell was rendered cracked more than once, and was rendered unringable in 1846 when rung on George Washington's birthday.
- Revolutionary War soldiers helped begin Independence Day celebrations across The United States by gathering on July 4th to remember war experiences.
- The *Pledge of Allegiance* first appeared in the Boston-based magazine *The Youth's Companion*, in 1892.

Literature Selections

Beat the Drum, Independence Day has Come: Poems for the Fourth of July by Lee B. Hopkins: Boyds Mills Press, 1993. (Picture book, 32 pg.) A compilation of short poems about fireworks, parades, and picnics.

Fireworks, Picnics, and Flags by James Cross Giblin: Houghton Mifflin, 1983 (Reference book, 90 pg.) Giblin's work is a spirited look at the history of America's Independence Day.

The Fourth of July Story by Alice Dalgliesh: Aladdin, 1995. (Picture book, 32 pg.) A children's version of the historical events leading up to the birth of a Nation.

Hurray for the Fourth of July by Wendy Watson: Houghton Mifflin, 2000. (Picture book, 32 pg.) A fun look at how a family in a small town spends Independence Day.

I Declare...

What does independence mean? Discuss how the *Declaration of Independence* proclaimed to the world that the United States of America was a free and independent country. Show a picture reference of the actual document, if possible. Talk about how independence means doing things on your own. Then, ask children to think of things they would like to learn to do independently, such as tying their shoes. On a sheet of parchment-colored stationery, write declarations of independence, telling about the things students will do. Use a feather dipped in ink to sign the declarations, then read them aloud.

INK

Pleased To Meet You, Uncle Sam!

Invite Uncle Sam to visit your classroom during the Fourth of July celebration. Explain that Uncle Sam is a character used to represent the United States in cartoons and drawings. Show pictures of Uncle Sam, if possible. Enlarge a hat pattern (page 81) and draw two shoe shapes on either red or blue construction paper. Cut out two mitten shapes for hands. Let each child follow the directions and diagram below to make an Uncle Sam. Hang the Uncle Sam crafts around the room for a bold, bright display.

1. Make pants by cutting a vertical slit in an 11" x 17" sheet of red construction paper. Glue long strips of white paper to the pants to create stripes.

2. Create a jacket by folding two sheets of blue construction paper in half, then gluing the folded sheets to the top of the pants, one on each side.

3. To add sleeves, cut two squares from blue paper, and glue them behind the back of the jacket.

4. Draw an Uncle Sam face on a paper plate, add a cotton ball beard, then glue the paper plate to the inside of the jacket. Add the hands and shoes. Copy and cut out the hat pattern on red paper, color the hat band blue, and glue the hat to the head. Decorate Uncle Sam's jacket with cut-out stars (see *How to Make a Five-Pointed Star*, page 63).

What Beautiful Fireworks!

Create a fireworks display indoors with these fun-to-make paintings. Provide sheets of dark blue construction paper, straws, and thinned tempera paint (thin the paint with water, then add a small amount of glue). Let each child choose a color of paint, place a small spoonful on the paper, then gently blow through the straw on top of the paint, spreading it out so that it resembles an exploding firecracker. Add other colors of "fireworks" to the paper skies. Sprinkle glitter over the wet paint. For added fun, tack the dry paintings to the ceiling so that children can look up and see fireworks during your Independence Day classroom celebration.

I Promise To Be Loyal

Even if students recite the *Pledge of Allegiance* every day, they may not know exactly what it means. Copy each line of the pledge onto a red, white, or blue sentence strip. Give each strip to a small group, along with a blank sentence strip of the same color. Provide dictionaries and other reference to help the groups determine what each line means. Copy the best explanation of each line onto a matching sentence strip. Display the sentence strips together, with the original version on the left and the new version on the right. Read the original lines and their meanings. Finally, let the class recite the new version of the pledge together.

An Ode to the Flag

Become a patriotic song writer in the tradition of Francis Scott Key, author of the American National Anthem. *The Star Spangled Banner* was originally a poem. Read and explain the lyrics of *The Star-Spangled Banner*. Draw the Stars and Stripes on a horizontal sheet of white paper, but do not color the stripes. On each stripe, write a word or phrase about the American flag, creating a flag poem. Color the flags after the poems have been completed, leaving the words legible. Then, post the flag poems around the flag in your classroom.

The flag is flying
At the baseball game.
Old Glory
Is its name.
We all stand up,
Everyone is still.
The music starts,
I wait until
Everyone else
Sings out loud.
I love my flag!
It makes me proud!

Stars and Stripes Everywhere!

Students will see stars and stripes forever while making these flag collages! Explain that the first flag had 7 red stripes and 6 white stripes, as well as 13 stars, to represent the 13 original colonies of the United States. Provide old magazines and instruct the class to cut out objects with either stripes or stars on them. Draw the outlines of stripes on large sheets of paper (do not color them in), glue the striped pictures across the paper (make sure the striped pictures alternate with white space), then put the starred pictures in the upper left corner to make the starred section. Attach the flags to wooden dowels, play some patriotic music, and let students march and proudly wave their flag collages.

Sparkling Streamers

Make your classroom stream with Fourth of July enthusiasm. Let each child glue glitter onto star patterns (page 81), then glue red and white paper streamers to the bottom of each star. Attach a craft stick to the back of each star, wave the streamers, and sing patriotic songs.

I wish all the people of America had enough to eat.

I wish all the people of America had nice parents like me.

I wish all people of America could see without glasses.

Wish Upon a Star

Get students thinking with the question: *If you could have one wish granted for all the people of America, what would it be?* Pass out enlarged star patterns (page 80) and have students write and illustrate their wishes on the stars. Place the patterns in a jar and draw a star each day, reading the wish aloud. Post the star on a bulletin board and write possible ways to grant the wish on smaller star patterns. Place them around the large star.

Proud Americans

Patriotism will fly high when your students express what freedom means to them. Explain that being patriotic means taking pride in the nation in which you live. Give each student handwriting paper and a copy of the flag pattern (page 80) enlarged to approximately the same size. Have students use their handwriting paper to record what freedom means and why they should be proud of their country. Provide markers or crayons, glitter, and foil stars for students to decorate their flags. Then, staple the flag patterns over the writing papers. Display the stories around the room.

I am proud to be an American because I am free to ride my bicycle and play with my friends.

77

Handy-Dandy Class Flag

Let each child lend a hand in making a cooperative class-sized flag. Pair children and have them trace several copies of each other's hands with the fingers spread slightly apart on red and blue paper. Make enough red hands for stripes and enough blue hands for the canton (blue part of the flag). Sketch a flag outline on a large sheet of white poster board and glue overlapping red hands onto the board in a stripe pattern. Glue a red stripe at the top and the bottom, and alternate the remaining stripes in between. Overlap the blue hands in the upper left corner, then add rows of white, sponge painted stars on top of the blue hands. Display the flag in the classroom to remind students that it took all of their helping hands to make it!

Festive Firecracker

Let children take home these shiny table toppers to use as centerpieces. Give each student a large spool (available at craft stores); red, white, blue, gold, or silver pipe cleaners; and large beads in the same colors. Paint the spools red, white, and blue, then place several pipe cleaners of different lengths into the hole in the center of each spool. Thread the beads onto the pipe cleaners at different heights, then bend the pipe cleaners outward to make a spray of firecracker colors. Create a festive Fourth environment by displaying the fireworks on students' desks. To continue the fireworks celebration, have the class complete the *Fourth of July Fun!* worksheet (page 79).

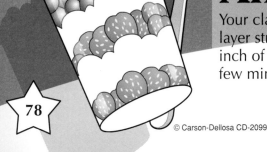

American Parfait

Your class will devour this star-spangled snack! In clear, plastic cups, layer strawberries and whipped topping to make stripes, leaving a $1/2$ inch of space at the top. Fill the cup with blueberries, then top with a few miniature marshmallows to represent stars. Enjoy!

FOURTH OF JULY FUN!

Word Bank

stars	flag	pledge
freedom	stripes	July

t _ _ p

ee

_ l _ g

_ ta _ _

l _ _ e

_ u _ y

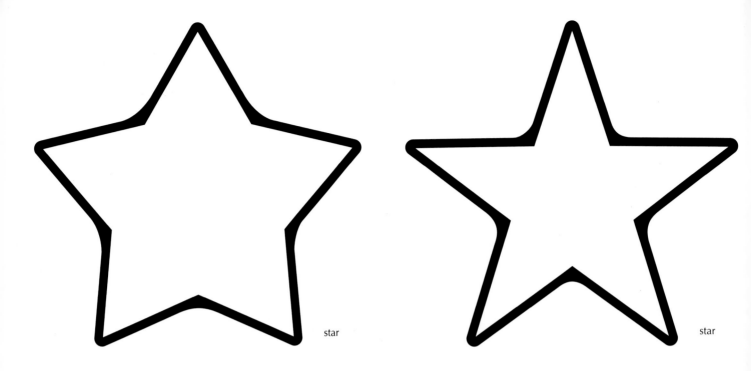

star

star

flag

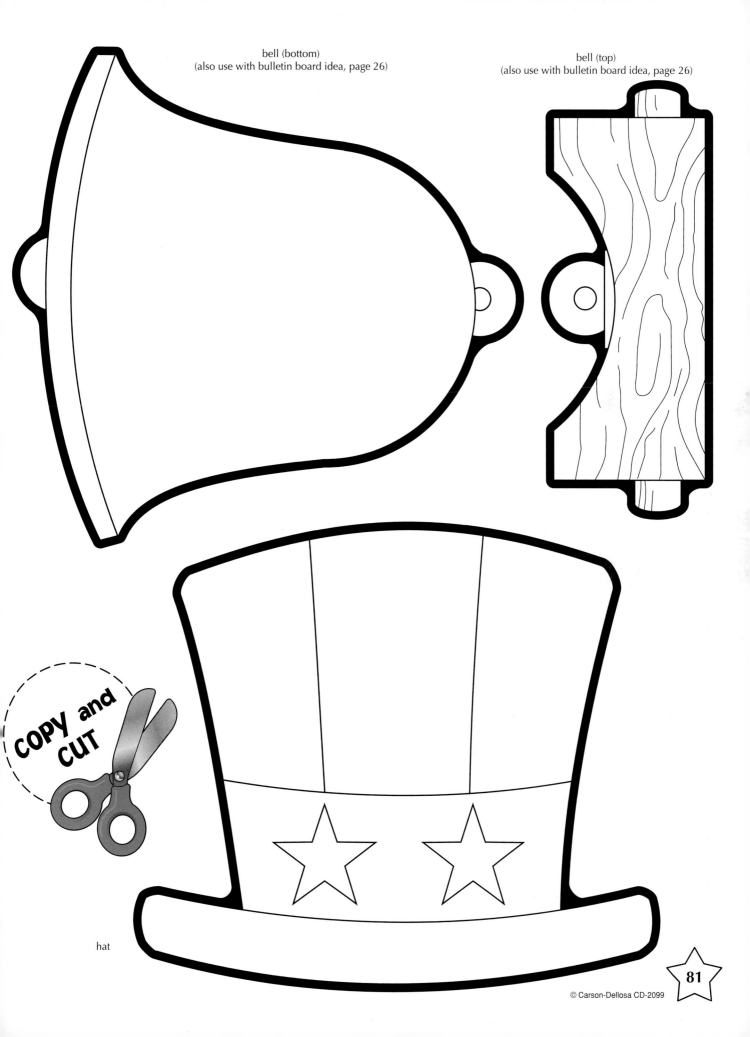

bell (bottom)
(also use with bulletin board idea, page 26)

bell (top)
(also use with bulletin board idea, page 26)

COPY and CUT

hat

Lovely Day For a Picnic

It's a bright, warm summer day—a perfect time for a picnic! Pack your baskets, grab your sun visors, and head outdoors for some picnic-centered fun.

Did You Know?

In the 1800s, a picnic was an indoor gathering where people brought their own food to eat.

Watermelons, a popular picnic food, are sometimes called *August hams* because of their size and the time they are harvested.

Ants, a common (and uninvited) picnic guest, can carry over 100 times their weight!

Literature Selections

● *Once Upon a Picnic* by Vivian French: Candlewick Press, 1996. (Storybook, 32 pg.) Characters from several fairy tales take a young boy on a picnic.

● *One Hundred Hungry Ants* by Elinor J. Pinczes: Houghton Mifflin, 1993. (Picture book, 32 pg.) A group of ants tries to come up with a new way to get to a picnic.

● *Picnic with Piggins* by Jane Yolen: Harcourt Brace, 1993. (Picture book, 32 pg.) A mystery develops during a relaxing picnic in the country.

● *Watermelon Day* by Kathi Appelt: Henry Holt & Co., 1996. (Picture book, 32 pg.) A little girl waits all summer for a watermelon to grow.

Bring Your Own Basket

Make picnic-perfect baskets for your class! Follow these steps to make picnic baskets from paper bags, then save the finished projects for a class picnic!

1. Cut off the top portion of a paper grocery bag.

2. Fold out the top edge of the bag to make a basket.

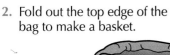

3. Cut a strip from the top half of the bag. Fold it in half lengthwise and staple it together. Staple it to the sides of the bag to make the handle.

4. Provide basket and ant patterns (page 85), construction paper, crayons, and markers, and let students decorate the baskets with outdoor scenes.

Sunny Day Visors

Let the sun shine brightly on your picnic, but keep it out of students' eyes with paper plate sun visors. Cut out the centers of white paper plates, leaving the rims intact. Let students place their plates on their heads to be sure that they fit. Cut several plates in half, and let students personalize them using markers and crayons. Staple each plate half to the rim, creating a sun visor. Let the class wear the visors for outdoor (or indoor) picnic activities.

Drink in the Picnic Fun!

Picnicking on a hot summer day can make for thirsty children. You bring the lemonade and let children bring the special picnic cups. Allow each student to use acrylic paint and small paintbrushes to add a design to a plastic cup. Make sure to paint only the bottoms and middles of the cups if they are used for drinking. On picnic day, bring lemonade made from a mix or from your favorite recipe for a refreshing way to cool off!

Pack Your Picnic Lunch

Pack your bags–lunch bags, that is–for a class picnic. Provide small paper lunch bags, several colors of paint poured onto paper plates, and sponges cut into picnic shapes. Gently press the sponges into the paint, then press the sponges onto the bags. Use markers to add details to the dry paint. Send finished bags home with notes explaining that children should pack picnic lunches from home in their bags for a class picnic.

A Place to Gather

What's a picnic without a blanket? Create a picnic blanket from a plain bedsheet. Spread the sheet over several layers of newspaper on top of a table. Let the class use fabric markers, fabric paint, shape sponges, and pieces of fabric and fabric glue to decorate the picnic "blanket." Copy the ant, basket, and watermelon slice patterns (page 85) onto oaktag to trace and color on the sheet. Use the finished blanket for picnics, storytime, independent reading, and small group activities.

83

© Carson-Dellosa CD-2099

A Place"mat" for a Picnic

Woven mats make any place a perfect place for a picnic. Have each child cut a sheet of construction paper into 2"-wide strips. Fold another, different-colored sheet of paper in half, and cut straight or wavy slits in the paper, beginning at the fold and stopping about 1" from the edge. Open the sheet of paper and weave the strips through the slits one at a time. Begin by weaving a strip first over, then under, then over, all the way to the edge. Weave the next strip under first, then over, etc. When all of the strips have been woven into the paper, glue the edges of the strips to the edge of the sheet of paper. Then, cut fringes along the edges to resemble a placemat. Finally, draw ants or picnic foods on the woven squares of the construction paper. Store the placemats in the picnic baskets from *Bring Your Own Basket* (page 82) and you'll always have a place for a picnic!

Icy Watermelon Pops

Here's a new idea for an old picnic favorite: watermelon pops! Bring a large watermelon to class and cut it into slices. Remove the seeds with craft sticks, (reserve them for *Ready, Set, Pinch!*, below). Scoop the melon out of the rind with a large ice cream scoop. Place a few scoops at a time into a blender and blend until the mixture is smooth. Fill paper cups with the blended watermelon and place them in a freezer. When the pops begin to freeze, place a craft stick in the center of each. Leave the treats in the freezer until they are completely frozen. Pop the "meloncicles" out of the paper cups for everyone to enjoy.

Ready, Set, Pinch!

Find a use for watermelon seeds and create a fun outdoor game at the same time! Treat the class to watermelon. Place the seeds in a small paper cup. (Be sure to play this game while the seeds are still slippery.) Place a plain sheet outside on a flat surface. Mark a chalk or tape line a few feet from the sheet. Let students stand on the line and pinch seeds until they pop out. Write each child's name on a piece of masking tape and place it on the sheet where her seed lands. When everyone has taken a turn, give a prize, such as an extra *Icy Watermelon Pop* (see above) or a piece of watermelon-flavored gum to the child whose seed went the farthest. Let students measure to find out how far the winning seed traveled.

On the Trail of an Ant

Let students use their writing skills to follow the paths of mischievous picnic ants. On butcher paper, have each student draw a picnic scene, complete with a hungry ant, picnic foods, a picnic basket, and a nearby anthill. Use a pencil to lightly draw a line from ant to anthill, going under, over, around, and near different objects in the picture. Then, following the path of the line, write a short story about where the ant must travel to get a morsel of food to its home, using as many position words (over, above, etc.) as possible. Let children read each others' stories and share in ant-chasing adventures.

84

ant

COPY and CUT

watermelon slice
(also use with bulletin board idea pg. 26)

basket
(also use with bulletin board idea pg. 27)

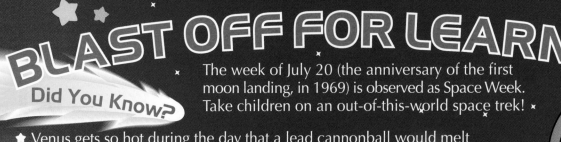

BLAST OFF FOR LEARNING!

The week of July 20 (the anniversary of the first moon landing, in 1969) is observed as Space Week. Take children on an out-of-this-world space trek!

★ Venus gets so hot during the day that a lead cannonball would melt on its surface!

★ Jupiter is so large that all of the other planets in the solar system could fit inside of it.

★ If the planet Saturn was put in a giant bathtub full of water, it would float.

★ The very first animal to travel in outer space was a Russian dog named Laika.

Literature Selections

★ *Astronauts Today* by Rosanna Hansen: Random House, 1998. (Picture book, 24 pg.) Color photographs accompany fun facts about space exploration.

★ *The Moon Book* by Gail Gibbons: Holiday House, 1997. (Picture book, 32 pg.) An easily understood book about the moon's phases and other interesting facts.

★ *Pluto: A Tour of the Solar System* by Loreen Leedy: Holiday House, 1993. (Picture book, 32 pg.) Colorful pictures take readers on a tour of the solar system.

★ *What's Out There?: A Book About Space* by Lynn Wilson: Price Stern Sloan Pub., 1993. (Picture book, 32 pg.) Answers many questions about space and the solar system.

Space Logs

During space travel, many astronauts keep a written record of their observations, experiences, and new discoveries. Throughout their studies about space, let your young astronauts keep space logs. To make a space log, have each child cover two letter-sized sheets of poster board with aluminum foil. Bind several sheets of writing paper between the foil covers by punching holes in the paper and covers and threading a paper clip through each hole. Glue on a title, then decorate the log with stars, planets, etc. Each day, let students use their logs to record exciting knowledge, list details from space adventures, and draw pictures of their observations.

86

My Stars

Is the Milky Way full of milk? No...it's full of stars! Help students understand that billions of stars make up our galaxy with this glittering galaxy collage. Copy the spiral galaxy pattern (page 91) and let each student cut out "spacy" pictures from catalogs (stars, planets, moons, the Earth, comets, etc.) to glue inside the spiral galaxy shape. Glue the entire shape to blue construction paper. Apply a thin coat of white glue to the spiral shape and the construction paper, and shake glitter over the collage. Challenge students to count the individual pieces of glitter, and draw a comparison to the billions of stars in the Milky Way. Reward students with a small Milky Way® candy bar, letting them use the wrappers as the titles for their collages.

Our Sun, the Star of Our Solar System

Your room will shine when you display bright ideas about the sun. Help each child follow these instructions to make a sun fact page. Trace a large circle onto a sheet of yellow and a sheet of orange construction paper, then trace another circle (about 1" smaller) inside the large yellow circle. Draw lines to divide the smaller, yellow circle into eight wedge-shaped sections. Cut along the straight part of the wedges, leaving the rounded edges attached to the yellow paper, to make eight fold-out "rays." Glue the edge of the yellow circle to the top of the orange circle, leaving the rays free. Fold back each ray and write a fact about the sun, then decorate the middle of the sun (under the rays on the orange paper) with a short poem.

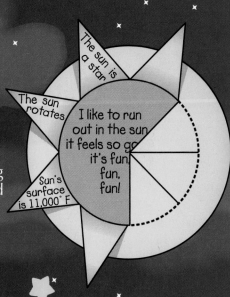

The sun is a star

The sun rotates

Sun's surface is 11,000° F

I like to run out in the sun it feels so go it's fun, fun, fun!

Preposterous Planetary Sentences

Make crazy classroom acrostics to remember all of the planets. Creating a silly sentence with the first letter of each planet is a good way to remember the planets' order from the sun. Show students the example at right, and instruct them to write the letters vertically on a page in their *Space Logs* (page 86), then write a word beside each letter so that it makes a silly sentence. Let students illustrate the sentences, then display them around the room.

M	Many
V	Very
E	Excited
M	Mice
J	Jumped
S	Slowly
U	Under
N	Navy
P	Pianos

87

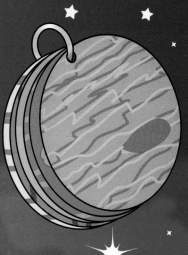

Paper Plate Planets

Get the planetary facts straight with these well-rounded planet booklets. Divide the children into nine groups and assign each group a planet. The groups should then present factual information to the class, and should describe how to make a paper plate look like their assigned planet. Provide all children with a paper plate before each presentation. During the presentation, tell students to write important facts about the planet on the back of the paper plate, then follow the group's instructions to color the front of the plate to resemble that group's planet. When all nine planet plates are finished, attach the edges of each set of plates with a loose leaf ring, so that one planet at a time can be referenced.

Planet Hopping

What better way to review the planets than by planet hopping? Draw nine large circles in a hop scotch pattern, and draw one large circle at the beginning. Label this circle *the sun*, and label the smaller circles with the names of planets. Play *Planet Hop Scotch*, but instead of jumping in numerical order, let students use an asteroid (small rock) as a marker to hop in planet order through the solar system. Challenge each player to name a fact about each planet as the "asteroid" lands on it.

Today's Forecast For Jupiter

Today: 100% chance of the Great Red Spot Hurricane continuing.
High: -101° F (-121°C).
Low: -238° F (-150° C)

Winds up to 400 miles per hour.
Tomorrow: Same.

How's the Weather Out There?

Children may be fascinated to learn how different the weather is on other planets! Divide the children into nine groups. Let the groups research the weather on each planet, and plan pretend weather forecasts to present to the class. Have each group choose someone to be the weather reporter, someone to make a forecast poster, and someone to compile research and list it as a forecast for the reporter to read. During each presentation, encourage the class to record information about each planet's weather and climate in their *Space Logs* (page 86).

Moon Changes

Get students' wheels spinning about the phases of the moon by making moon wheels. For the bottom of the wheel, trace a large circle onto white paper. Divide it into eight equal wedges. Use this circle to trace and cut out another circle (the top of the wheel), and cut one wedge out of it that is slightly smaller than the wedges from the divided circle. Cut out copies of the moon phase patterns (page 92) and glue them in order, one in each section, around the wheel. Label the patterns with the phases. Place the top wheel over the bottom wheel, and attach them at the center with a brad to create a device to show the moon's phases over and over again. Turn the top of the wheel to the phase that is showing that night, then adjust the wheel about twice each week to keep up with the changes of the moon. Check a lunar calendar to see when the phases are occurring. The moon will change from full to new in about two weeks. Report lunar observations during the morning calendar routine and let students record the dates and moon phases in their *Space Logs* (page 86). As an alternative to individual wheels, consider keeping a large version of the phase wheel on a bulletin board, or tracking the moon phases over the month on a posted calendar.

Moon Walk

If you walked on the moon, your footprints would last forever because there is no wind or rain on the moon to destroy them. Have students pretend to walk on the moon where there is almost no gravity, then write about the experience in their *Space Logs* (page 86). Make lasting moon footprints like astronauts Neil Armstrong and Buzz Aldrin. Let students wear old shoes, dip their feet in gray paint, then carefully step on a large sheet of paper. Paint craters around the footprints. Tape the footprints in a line across a bulletin board to create a moon walk!

Suspended Satellites

Satellites (objects that orbit around planets) are visible and useful in our everyday lives. The moon is a natural satellite. Man-made satellites help people gather and transmit data around the world. Design artificial satellites from pint-sized milk cartons. Paint a milk carton and then insert a pipe cleaner through the center of the carton so that an equal amount of pipe cleaner extends from either side. Create panels by covering construction paper rectangles with aluminum foil, then gluing two to each end of the pipe cleaner. Hang the satellites from the ceiling. Research and record information which might be received from satellites, such as weather data, television transmissions, or telephone communications.

89

Guest Speaker, John Glenn!

Introduce your class to important figures in the history of space travel. Provide books and information about space travelers such as Laika (first dog to travel in outer space), Sally Ride (first American woman in space), and John Glenn (first U.S. astronaut to circle the Earth and the oldest man in space). Then, let each child make a space puppet from a lunch-sized paper bag. Staple a paper flap to the paper bag, select an astronaut or space traveler, then write facts about the traveler under the flaps. Decorate the puppet to look like the traveler. Children may also wish to make spaceship puppets in addition to their people. Finally, have each puppet become a "guest speaker." (Animal and spaceship travelers can speak, too!) Lift the flaps to show facts as the speakers relate their autobiographies to the class. Encourage children to take notes about the speakers in their *Space Logs* (page 86).

3,2,1, BLAST OFF!

Children can give these homemade rockets all the "blast" they need to sail across space. Have each child roll a half-sheet of lightweight paper into a tube, then secure the overlap with tape. Trace a circle, about 5" in diameter, onto the other sheet, then cut it out, roll it into a cone shape and secure it with tape. Tape the cone to the tube on opposite sides. Decorate the rocket and tape red and orange strips cut from paper streamers to the bottom. Go outside and have a class countdown. (Make sure students aim away from others at launching time.) To launch a rocket, place it on top of a drinking straw. Let the rocket rest on the straw and blow forcefully into the straw. Watch those rockets fly!

Let's Take a Rocket Trip!

Enjoy this outer-space adventure over and over again! Let students write a story about a trip on a rocket ship. Then, fold over the top third of a large sheet of black construction paper and staple the story under the resulting flap. Draw a horizontal, wavy line across the middle of the remaining length of construction paper, stopping about 1 1/2" from each edge. Cut on the line to make a wavy slit in the paper. Then, cut out and decorate two circles, one to represent the Earth and the other to represent the other planet or satellite in the story. Glue the Earth and the other planet to opposite ends of the slit. Finally, cut out and color a rocket ship pattern (page 91), and glue it onto the end of a craft stick. Insert the craft stick into the slit, and move the craft stick across the paper. Take turns reading stories and "traveling" in the attached rocket ships!

90

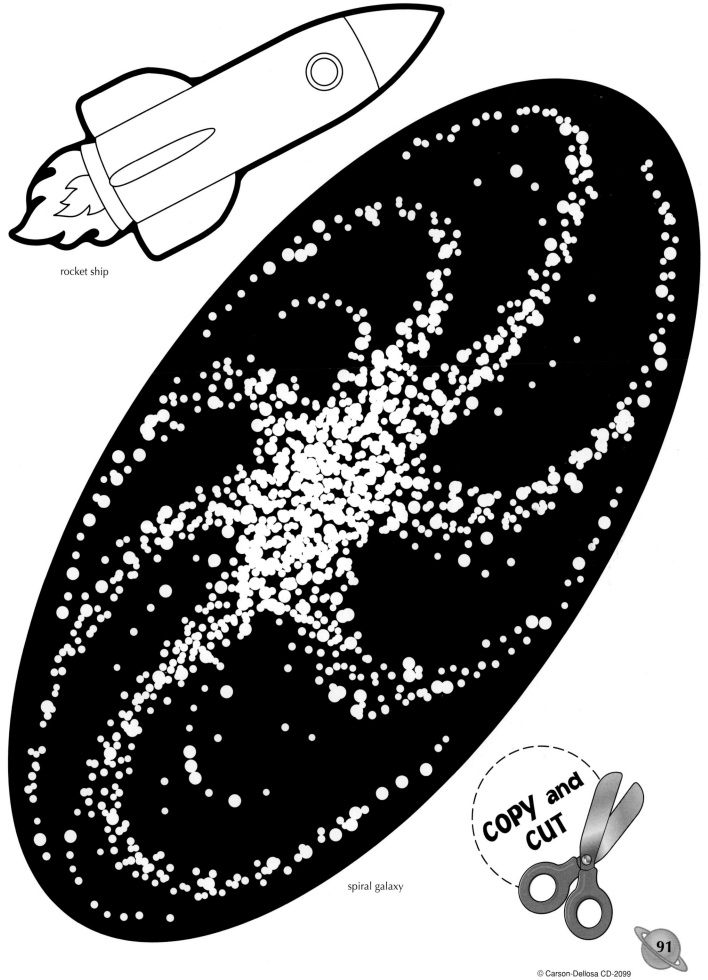

rocket ship

spiral galaxy

COPY and CUT

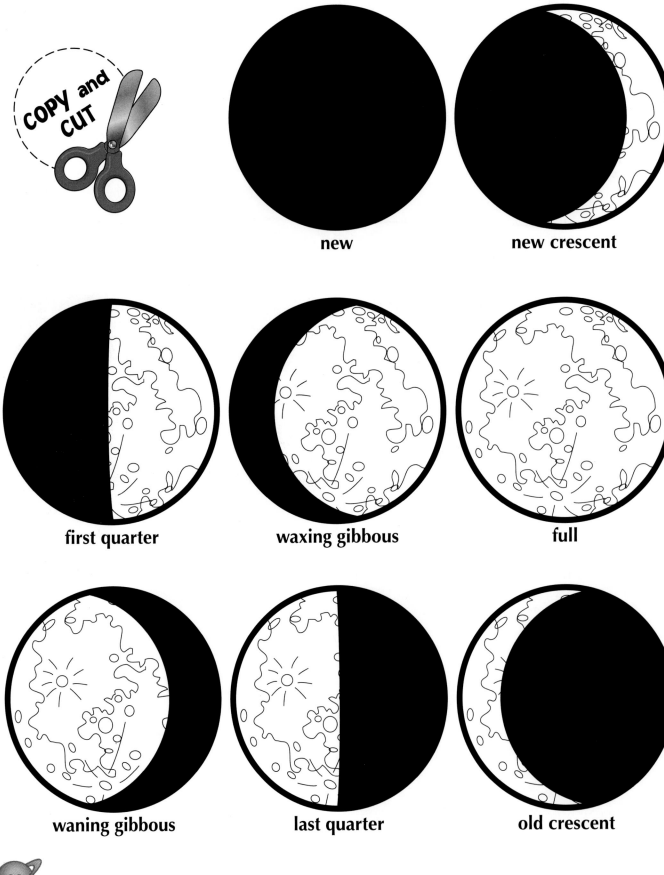

COPY and CUT

new

new crescent

first quarter

waxing gibbous

full

waning gibbous

last quarter

old crescent

INTERNATIONAL Holidays

Dragon Boat Festival

Every year on the fifth day of the fifth lunar moon, usually in late June or early July, the Chinese celebrate the Dragon Boat Festival. This celebration is an important one, and has the longest history of all the holidays in China. The holiday started as a time for driving away evil spirits and for finding peace in one's life. Later, the legend of Chu Yuan, a patriotic poet who lived over 2,000 years ago, was added to the festivities. Chu Yuan drowned in a river. According to legend, fishermen tried to save the poet by sailing in their boats and looking for him. Today, boats in the shape of dragons are raced along rivers in many parts of China. Teams row their boats and a drumbeat is played to keep their rowing in time. People dress in their best clothes to watch the races and eat *tzungtzu* (rice dumplings wrapped in bamboo leaves).

Patriotic Poem
by Jennifer W.

Gently rolling hills
and skies of blue
mountains so tall
and smiling people, too!

Patriotic Poems

Talk with the class about what it means to be patriotic and what kinds of things Chu Yuan might have written about his country in his poetry, such as the beauty of the land, the kindness of the people, etc. See if students can name existing patriotic songs, poems, etc. Then, have students write patriotic poems about their country. Post the completed poems on a bulletin board or wall.

Float Your Boat

Make your own festive dragon boats with shoeboxes, construction paper, markers, wrapping paper, tissue paper, etc. Have students create models of boats they would like to see in the Dragon Boat Festival. Punch a hole in the front of each boat. Provide students with a 3'-long piece of string. Instruct students to tie a string to each hole. Allow students to have "boat races" by pulling their new art creations across the classroom floor!

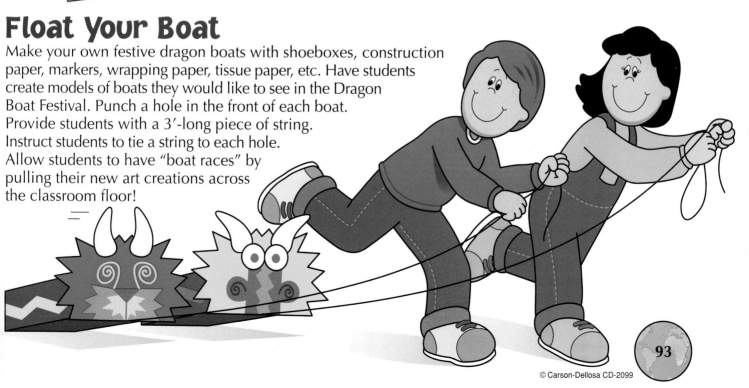

93

Dragon Boat Festival (continued)
Hooray for Sachets!

The Dragon Boat Festival is a time to think of peace and health. Children wear colorful sachets during the celebration because it is believed that they bring peace and good luck. Provide each student with a 6" square piece of light-colored cloth. Then, supply permanent markers, beads, glue, etc., and allow students to decorate their sachets any way they choose. After the sachets have dried, provide students with cloves or potpourri to place in their sachets. Have students wrap the cloth around the cloves or potpourri and tie with string, leaving some cloth above the string. Then, punch holes in opposite sides of the sachet's top. Supply each student with a 12" piece of colorful ribbon. Have them thread the ribbon through each hole, then knot the ribbon so students are able to wear their sachets around their necks.

Keep the Beat!

It is customary during the Dragon Boat Festival for drums to be played during the race. Allow students to make their own drums to play while racing the boats they made in the *Float Your Boat* activity (page 93). Provide two rounded, empty containers, such as oatmeal containers, for each child. Let students decorate two pieces of brown construction paper. Wrap one piece of the paper around each container. Have students lightly tap the tops of their "drums" with their fingers.

Dragon Boat Festival Greeting Cards

Have students make Dragon Boat Festival greeting cards to give to friends or relatives. Give each student a large piece of construction paper to fold in half, lengthwise. Have students draw dragon boats on the outsides of their cards and tape red curling ribbon to their dragon mouths to represent fire. On the inside, have each student write a Dragon Boat Festival message, such as *Wishing you peace and good health in your life.*

Canada Day

July 1 in Canada marks the creation of the Canadian federal government in 1867, and since 1982 has been known as Canada Day. Before 1982, it was known as Dominion Day, First of July, and July the First. It is Canada's national independence celebration, much like the Fourth of July in the United States. Canada Day is a time to spend with family and friends and to celebrate Canadian heritage. Canada Day is celebrated in many different ways. Picnics, barbecues, and fireworks displays are popular activities.

Canadian Fact Flags

Making fact flags is a good way to teach students a little about Canada. Provide reference books about Canada. Ask each student to write one fact about the country, such as *The French pioneered the first European settlement in Canada*. Then, give each student a piece of white construction paper, two red strips of construction paper about 2" wide, and a red construction paper maple leaf. Instruct students to copy their facts on the maple leaves. Let students glue the red construction paper strips to each end of the white construction paper. Next, students can glue the maple leaves in the middle. Finally, supply each student with a craft stick to glue to the back of her flag. Let students wave their flags and knowledge around!

The French pioneered the first European settlement in Canada.

O Canada!

In honor of Canada Day, teach students the first verse of *O Canada*, the Canadian national anthem. The English lyrics to the anthem were written by Robert Stanley Weir in 1908.

O Canada!
Our home and native land!
True patriot love in all thy sons command.
With glowing hearts we see thee rise,
Our True North strong and free!
From far and wide, O Canada!
We stand on guard for thee.

95

Bastille Day

Bastille (ba•STEEL) Day (July 14) is a national holiday in France. It marks the storming of a French prison, the Bastille, which occurred in 1789. This event was the beginning of the French Revolution, which ultimately ended monarch rule and established the country as a Republic. Every year, the French celebrate this holiday with parades, fireworks, and merrymaking, much like Americans celebrate the Fourth of July.

A Brilliant Display

On July 14, there is a magnificent fireworks display in many French cities. Create a colorful tribute to France on Bastille Day. Provide each student with a piece of white construction paper, and blue, red, and black crayons. Fold the construction paper into thirds, lengthwise. On the left third of the paper, have students cover the area with a heavy layer of blue. Next, have them cover the right third with a heavy layer of red. Now students have a replica of the French flag. Next, instruct students to cover the entire piece of construction paper with a heavy layer of black crayon. Provide each student with a coin or paper clip and instruct her to scratch a firework pattern into the black crayon layer so the bright colors show through. As a finishing touch, have students carve a birthday message to France underneath the fireworks display.

Great Crepes

Make students' mouths water by making traditional French crepes on Bastille Day! The American breakfast pancake is a version of this French dessert. To save time, prepare the crepes the night before, then add the toppings in class.

Batter:
Mix 1½ cups of sifted flour, 1 tablespoon of sugar, and ½ teaspoon of salt in a medium mixing bowl. Next, stir in ½ teaspoon vanilla, 2 eggs, beaten, and 1 tablespoon of oil. Add 2 cups of milk, ¼ cup at a time. The mixture should be very thin. Cover and refrigerate until you are ready to use the batter.

To prepare the crepes:
Butter a frying pan. Heat on medium until the butter starts to bubble. Pour in ¼ cup of the batter. Rotate the pan so the batter is spread out in the pan. Cook about 30 seconds and turn over. Cook an additional 20 seconds.

Top the crepes with fruit, ice cream, powdered sugar, or enjoy them plain! If there are extra crepes, place them between two sheets of wax paper and freeze. Let crepes thaw at room temperature for one hour before serving.